HOUSES

HOUSES

EXTRAORDINARY
LIVING

It may be a cliché, but it's absolutely true. Of all building types, the house is the most personal and the most essential. Our home is our sanctum, and it is a mirror on our private selves. For architects, it's the place to most freely experiment and, often, to establish a reputation before moving on to larger-scale projects. For historians, residential design is a bellwether—a forerunner of changes in style, philosophy, and technique. Exceptional houses have changed and shaped architectural history, and they have long influenced how and where we live, and even how our societies function.

The four hundred homes in this book—visually paired to provide imaginative space for the reader to make their own connections— are a cross section of the most remarkable residential achievements of the modern era, from the beginning of the twentieth century to the present. The selection includes everything from small prefabs to vast estates, in styles ranging from Art Nouveau and Arts and Crafts to Modernism, High-Tech, postmodernism, Deconstructivism, Neo-Modernism, and styles that are emerging now. These houses are landmarks of architectural innovation: levitating masses, concrete and fiberglass prototypes, radically open layouts, and abodes that have an easy relationship with the landscape. They chart constant shifts in taste, style, and thought.

Some are international icons. Others have become synonymous with their architectural styles and their times. Many more are hidden revelations created by talents left off the usual lists. Each represents an important light in the complex constellation of twentieth- and twenty-first-century residential architecture. They exist along a fixed timeline—indeed, at the end of the book there is a section showing the houses in chronological order—but their progression is by no means linear. Some of the most forward-looking homes were constructed at the birth of the twentieth century. Conversely a collection of recent projects celebrates the past, and the local, albeit with a modern twist.

In their own way, each house here represents fundamentally human values and aspirations. It's such aspirations that make the architects featured in this book, and their clients, most noteworthy.

Evolving Visions

The design movements that classify this kaleidoscope of exceptional homes help us make sense of their vastly varied formal, technical, and philosophical underpinnings—essentially charting their progress through architectural history.

Built at the turn of the twentieth century, Belgian master Victor Horta's own house (1901) p. 262 in Brussels, with its lacy metalwork, curving glass, and flowerlike murals, is a flourishing emblem of Art Nouveau, in which fluid lines of intricate decoration merge with structure and new materials in vividly depicting the natural world. Greene & Greene's rustic yet elegant Gamble House in Pasadena, California (1908) p. 67, with its exposed beams, puzzlelike joinery, integrated furniture, and sumptuous use of wood, dexterously epitomizes the Arts and Crafts movement, joining decorative and fine arts, traditional craft, and architecture as a reaction to the numbing uniformity of industrial production.

Coexisting with these novel forms were more familiar ones: historical styles like Mission Revival, Italianate, Neoclassical, and Beaux-Arts, that celebrated grandeur, ornament, and tradition. Finished two decades after it began, Julia Morgan's Hearst Castle (1947) p. 334 in San Simeon, California, resembles an eclectic and opulent Spanish mission, with rolling red tile, white surfaces, flamboyant carvings, bell towers, and rounded forms. Francis Burrall Hoffman's breathtaking Vizcaya (1922) p. 97, in Coconut Grove in Miami, Florida, resembles a Renaissance Italian villa, with its Classical and Baroque motifs, and lavish geometric gardens.

The early twentieth century also ushered in Neo-Plastic, Expressionist, and Constructivist residences, fluidly merging abstract art, design, and architecture. Stunning specimens include Gerrit Rietveld's Schröder House (1924) p. 390 in Utrecht, The Netherlands, with its sliding panels and bold blocks of color, and Konstantin Melnikov's own house (1929) p. 400 in Moscow, featuring ingeniously moving parts and strange honeycomb forms. Art Deco and Streamline Moderne residences express strong geometric patterns and dizzying vertical and horizontal movement. Robert Mallet-Stevens's Villa Noailles (1932) p. 185 in Hyères, France carves out a fashionable combination of staggered and fluid forms, while Josef Hoffmann's Palais Stoclet (1911) p. 273 in Brussels combines the massing and sumptuousness of a palace with the hard lines and flat edges of commercial machinery.

The ultimate embodiment of the modern industrial world was the emergence of Modernist architecture, marked by rejection of the past, abolition of ornament, easy replication, and an embrace of futuristic technology. One of its earliest iterations is the Steiner House (1910) p. 56, a white concrete, cubic form in Vienna created by Adolf Loos, who famously called ornament a "crime," not only as a waste of time and effort, but also as a symptom of immorality. Walter Gropius, a cofounder of the Bauhaus in Dessau, Germany, created the highly rational Masters' Houses (1926) p. 285, showcasing interlocking cubic structures, generous balconies, and (to some extent) modular construction.

The movement found its road map with the most famous Modernist house of all: Villa Savoye (1930) p. 68 in Poissy, France, a machine-inspired sculpture instilled with Le Corbusier's "five points of architecture," a regimented building prescription that called for pilotis, open plans, ribbon windows, free facades, and flat roof terraces. There was a flood of Modernist homes that followed, and a symbol of the movement's maturity—and adoption by the elite classes—was Mies van der Rohe's Farnsworth House (1951) p. 236, an icon of the International Style in Plano, Illinois. Mies stripped away ornament in favor of a sophisticated, elongated glass-and-steel box, both rising above and infusing itself with the idyllic landscape around it. The steel-framed California homes of Arts & Architecture's Case Study House Program—such as Pierre Koenig's Stahl House (1960) p. 192 and Charles and Ray Eames's Eames House (1949) p. 270; Case Study Houses No. 22 and No. 8 respectively—attempted to bring this minimal aesthetic to the masses; the emphasis was on affordability and off-the-shelf parts, helping disseminate midcentury panache worldwide.

Modern homes emerged in a phantasmagoria of varieties: the organic residences of Frank Lloyd Wright, Bruce Goff, and Herb Greene; the space-age creations of John Lautner and Luigi Moretti; the unadorned brutalist structures of Dale Naegle and Takamitsu Azuma; the classically inspired new formalist homes of Edward Killingsworth and Edward Durell Stone; and the overscaled, tech-driven late Modern concoctions of Arthur Erickson and Team 4. By the late 1960s and '70s, fatigue with Modernism's mass-produced aesthetic and ultra-serious ethos had spurred unusual, often irrational remedies. The postmodern cavalry was led by the likes of Robert Venturi (who together with Denise Scott Brown formed Venturi, Scott Brown, & Associates)—the Vanna Venturi House (1964) p. 407 in Chestnut Hill, Philadelphia, which Venturi designed for his mother, deliberately thumbs its nose at the Modernist movement's sacred tenets of progress and order. It references classical shapes and concepts including crowning pediments and axial symmetry, and does so using oversized and cartoonish elements. Venturi's contemporary Leon Krier, another leader of this new wave, emphasized historical regionalism, integrating the vernacular of the Florida panhandle into his own home (1987) p. 205 in Seaside, Florida, which integrates white clapboard siding, pitched roofs, and even a picket fence. Just as playful as the Vanna Venturi House, the home rises high in the air, culminating in a "temple" top, stretching a familiar vernacular into something altogether different.

Diverse offshoots sprang up, from the airy, coolly rational Neo-Modernism of Richard Meier, to the anarchic ebullience of Frank Gehry. Such stylistic fragmentation has only accelerated, in large part due to light-speed technical advances and global influences. Contemporary residences often embrace the minimalism of Modernism, such as David Chipperfield's Villa Eden (2015) p. 184, which inserts itself into the hilly topography of Gardone, Italy, through sublimely simple cube-shaped masses. Others incorporate super-graphics, digitally fabricated expressions, and even emojis. Moon Hoon's Wind House (2015) p. 147, for instance, sprouts a cartoonish curving, gold-hued tower from its rectilinear base, reminiscent of an alien or a duck. Elsewhere, lessons of regionalism and historicism inform sleek, understated creations. John Wardle Architects' Shearer's Quarters (2011) p. 324 in Tasmania, Australia, is clad in corrugated iron, evoking local sheds, with a pine interior inspired by apple crates. This house's angular, dramatically shifting form is all about the future. From this, one thing is clear: perhaps the only overriding residential philosophy today is that there is none?

Waves of Invention

Beyond style or even philosophy, the driving force behind most of these residential touchstones has been innovation. Houses have always served as test beds for technological, material, and spatial advances that have revolutionized how we construct and how we live.

From a bird's-eye view, we can observe the most basic progressions: proficiency with factory-tested industrial materials such as steel, cast iron, tile, reinforced concrete, and glass helped Art Nouveau come to life, made Beaux-Arts grander, and let the geometric maneuverings of Art Deco and Streamline Moderne thrive. Experiments in open plans, frame construction, modular techniques, and the mass production of glass, steel, and concrete, particularly after World War II, helped Modernist architecture expand from a niche into the dominant force of the midcentury. In the wake of Modernism, architects took advantage of a widened material palette, more systematized construction, and emerging digital technologies to build new, often quasi-sculptural forms. Digital design has since advanced exponentially, and we're beginning to see residences that have been designed algorithmically and fabricated robotically.

Whether taking on a project for themselves or a client, the architects featured in this book delighted in testing a home's most basic building block: structure. Perhaps most famously, Wright pushed the scope of the cantilever with Fallingwater (1939) p. 130, which thrust three steel-reinforced concrete floors perilously far from a stone base, hovering directly over a waterfall in Bear Run, Pennsylvania. Ensamble Studio's more recent Hemeroscopium House (2008) p. 338 in Madrid stacks cantilevered, concrete-clad I-beams in a grid, highlighted by a thin pool that stretches 65½ feet (20 meters) from the home itself.

Other houses more closely resemble infrastructure than architecture. The rusted-steel Shadowcliff house (1969) p. 157, designed by Harry Weese, hangs from metal beams over Lake Michigan in Ellison Bay, Wisconsin. Marcos Acayaba's Residencia

Olga (1990) p. 241 in São Paulo forms an inverted ziggurat, footed by sunken concrete columns supporting a steadily expanding wooden frame. In Zapallar, Chile, Undurraga Deves's Houses of the Horizon (2009) p. 339 encompass two truss-supported structures, which span large cavities excavated into a stone cliff.

Often structural experiments are disguised but no less effective. Eero Saarinen's Miller House (1957) p. 32 in Columbus, Indiana, achieves its column-free lightness by tying four separate buildings together with a skylit metal roof. The Villa Spies (1969) p. 45 in Torö, Sweden, designed by Staffan Berglund, is "supported" by clear glass walls—akin to a futuristic Maison de Verre (1932) p. 282—thanks to a hidden steel frame and a structural, rounded concrete roof.

More houses in this book exhibit a determined emphasis on material experiment. Steel-reinforced concrete, a vital tool throughout twentieth-century architecture, became an advanced testing ground as the century pressed on, pushed to the limits by Claude Parent, who had advocated "the death of the vertical line." His Maison Drusch (1965) p. 398 in Versailles and Bordeaux-Le Pecq House (1966) p. 77 in Bois-le-Roi, France, take on radically curved and canted profiles that presaged Deconstructivism by around two decades. About fifty years later, Charles Wright Architects employed a novel combination of poured-in-place and precast concrete to levitate its space-age Stamp House (2013) p. 63 in several directions over a native wetland in Queensland, Australia. Shigeru Ban, always the experimenter, utilized 110 cardboard tubes as structural members for his Paper House (1995) p. 209 in Lake Yamanaka, Japan, a test he went on to employ at a much larger scale globally.

Many visionaries experimented with manipulating space. Modern architects like Wright, with his revolutionary Robie House (1910) p. 79 in Chicago, Illinois, transformed cellular residences into open ones, allowing space to flow freely and removing walls formerly needed for practical reasons. California Modern homes, including Richard Neutra's Kaufmann Desert House (1947) p. 243, used pinwheel-shaped plans to encourage flow and to expose as many frontages as possible to their beautiful surroundings. Italian Modernist Carlo Scarpa arranged the fluid concrete forms of his Villa Ottolenghi (1978) p. 12, in Verona, to fan out into the landscape, creating a highly orchestrated progression toward lush gardens and pools. Kouichi Kimura's House of Silence (2012) p. 410 in Shiga, Japan, has a fortresslike exterior; in striking contrast, the interiors are bright and open, thanks to multiple inner courtyards and split-level rooms with varying ceiling heights.

Some experiments push beyond the house itself, into the landscape, creating new typologies. Joshua Schweitzer's The Monument (1990) p. 144 in Joshua Tree, California, comprises multiple structures dotting a site, utilizing the outdoors as a corridor. Hillside residences, such as Harwell Hamilton Harris's Weston Havens House (1941) p. 168 in San Francisco, use steel frames and deeply driven steel piles to float and flow over steep slopes. Future Systems' Malator House (1994) p. 191 is burrowed into a cliff in Wales; a plywood roof is camouflaged with grass, with only one ellipse-shaped glass frontage opening to the sea.

On a macro scale, Joseph Eichler's Eichler Homes p. 321 of the 1950s and '60s, in the San Francisco Bay area, developed a repeatable post-and-beam prototype—opening to a private inner courtyard—to bring Modernism to the everyman. It was an experiment that yielded more than eleven thousand residences in communities nationwide. Buckminster Fuller attempted a mass-producible Dymaxion prototype, with his aluminum, spaceship-shaped Wichita House (1946) p. 133 in Kansas, and Finnish architect Matti Suuronen created the prefabricated Futuro House (1968) p. 215, which resembles a UFO.

Influencers

Significant homes such as those profiled in this book have played a crucial role in defining how we live—setting the tone, and providing groundwork, for original residences. Modern pioneer Otto Wagner, employing new materials and forms while (very) loosely drawing from historical precedents and symbolic references, paved the way for countless architects hoping to break the shackles of historicism and inject a new vision into their work. His residences, like many products of the Vienna Secession, also helped launch a wave of mass publicity. They were artfully reproduced in posters, photographs, and books, displayed in museum and gallery exhibitions, and shown off (and often criticized) in new publications, including *Moderne Architektur* and *Der Architekt*. They played a major role in the emergence of the architect's so-called Wagner School, influencing the likes of Hoffmann, Josef Olbrich, Rudolph Schindler, and Louis Sullivan.

Wright (whose protégés fanned out to all corners of the globe) excelled at self-promotion, harnessing media including books, magazines, and, later, television to not just promote his work but also establish a unique persona and mythology. The success of his Prairie and Usonian Homes, with their open plans, horizontal focus, novel construction techniques (like slab foundations and underfloor heating), and close connection to their surroundings, influenced generations of residential designers, particularly in the rush to build housing after World War II. Similarly, Philip Johnson, a well-connected blue-blood with a knack for galvanizing attention, helped make his Glass House (1949) p. 212 in New Canaan, Connecticut—itself infamously influenced by Mies van der Rohe's Farnsworth House (1951) p. 236—into an architectural icon, hyped in both architecture periodicals like *Architectural Review* and consumer publications like *Life* magazine. *New York Times* architecture critic Nicolai Ouroussoff wrote in 2007 that the home's "celebrity may have done more to make Modernism palatable to the country's social elites than any other structure of the twentieth century."

The postmodern works of Krier, Michael Graves, Charles Jencks, Charles Moore, and Robert Venturi and Denise Scott Brown, with their cheeky nods to history and kitsch, have influenced a generation of homes that casually mimicked styles that generally had no place in their new surroundings.

Today's most exceptional contemporary homes continue to shape the residential landscape, far ahead of their imitators. They are disseminated more widely, and rapidly, than ever, via the Internet and social media. These exceptional residences, and their architects, are leaders, not followers. Their designs draw from collaboration—a synthesis of client, site, and personal vision—setting a new standard of invention.

As home building becomes more commodified, and values shift from design inspiration and quality of life to quantity of space and lists of amenities, luxury has, to a great extent, leapfrogged other considerations of contemporary taste. But it is rarely the driving force for the best homes. A truly extraordinary residence doesn't rely on gimmicks, formulas, or opulence. It's a deeply personal endeavor, emerging from the mind, heart, and soul of its architect, that inherently enhances and reflects its surroundings and the life of its occupants.

Sam Lubell

VILLA OTTOLENGHI, 1978

Verona, Italy

CARLO SCARPA

As in the work of Frank Lloyd Wright, to whom Scarpa is often compared, the structural elements of this house appear like the strata of natural rock, as demonstrated in the columns of alternating rings of colored natural stone and smooth polished concrete, shown here. The plan of the house is hinged on a series of nine of these columns, arranged in three clusters, from which groups of rooms fan out toward the landscape, each with its own separate series of views of the gardens, pools, and roof terraces set into a vineyard above Lake Garda. Scarpa's method of work is such that each event is separately conceived, and studied, and related to the whole loosely and thematically (rather than formally). This gives rise to buildings which are hard to understand from plans or photographs, but offer the visitor a succession of delights.

O HOUSE, 2007

Lucerne, Switzerland

PHILIPPE STUEBI ARCHITEKTEN

Zurich-based Philippe Stuebi Architekten designed this L-shaped house on a plot jutting out into Lake Lucerne. The extroverted mansion features a white concrete facade on the street side, which is perforated by giant cut-out circles, giving it a slightly brutalist sensibility and allowing tantalizing glimpses into the two-level orangery filled with exotic plants. On the lake side of the building there is a cantilevering loggia on the first floor, entered via the bedrooms, made from glass bricks—again circular. Superb views of the Rigi mountain, which J. M. W. Turner immortalized in paint three times, can be had from the sleek, minimalist living room. The basement boasts an underground gym, a half-inside, half-outside swimming pool, and a car park with a circular skylight not unlike that of Rome's Pantheon.

NASU TEPEE, 2013

Nasu, Tochigi, Japan

HIROSHI NAKAMURA & NAP

A primeval form of dwelling, a tent provides a sense of security, coziness, and proximity to the outdoors. A nature-loving couple wanted a weekend retreat in a wood in Tochigi Prefecture in Japan, an area well known as a summer resort, on a small footprint to avoid clearing too many trees. The chosen design resembles five pointed tents huddling together. Tall, pointed roofs maximize light, which enters through triangular windows at the apex of each pyramid. Sitting areas and beds are by walls, where the ceiling is lowest, to save space, and the small quarters encourage an intimate sociability. Rising warm air is either redistributed by vents to ground level in winter or released through windows in summer. The home's form echoes the grass-covered pit houses of the Jomon, a prehistoric Japanese people.

WILD BIRD, 1957

San Francisco, California, USA

NATHANIEL OWINGS
& MARK MILLS

Wild Bird enjoys a spectacularly lofty position 2,000 feet (600 meters) up on the cliffs at Grimes Point, Big Sur, overlooking the Pacific Ocean—*Time* magazine reported that "admirers call it the most beautiful house on the most beautiful site in the US." The name is apt, for red-tailed hawks can be seen swooping here, and the house's triangular A-frame form resembles the wings of a bird about to take flight. It is constructed of reclaimed redwood and concrete, and features linear skylights which allow sunshine into the open-plan living and kitchen area. Nathaniel Owings was a partner in Skidmore, Owings & Merrill. He and his soon-to-be wife, Margaret, found the spot in 1952 and resolved to make a home there. It would become, he said, "a onetime house for the rest of the time we expect to be here on earth."

HOUSE A AT WHIPSNADE, 1936

Whipsnade, England, UK

BERTHOLD LUBETKIN

As this house was for himself, Lubetkin took the opportunity to experiment. It was designed for maximum outdoor living, and built on a platform cut into the hill to make the most of the views. The bedrooms are provided with outdoor sleeping porches, and there is also an outdoor fireplace. Lubetkin was not a strict functionalist and he worked in an intuitive way, as demonstrated in the two highly expressive curved elements of the building. First, on the roof is an extended parabolic screen which, below, makes a room-within-a-room for dining; second, the entrance is screened by a semicircular "sun-catch." Lubetkin came to England in 1931 and set up Tecton (1932–48); although he is best known for the Penguin Pool (1934) at London Zoo, his deeply held socialist views led him to focus most of his career on public housing.

LOTUS HOUSE, 2005

Kamakura, Kanagawa, Japan

KENGO KUMA & ASSOCIATES

Lotus House is a quiet mountain residence designed as a weekend getaway from the city. A pool next to the home is filled with lotus flowers, which flow into it from a nearby river. Although the house's plan is relatively simple—two wings connected by a double-height courtyard—its facade is complex: its checkerboard pattern is made of a lattice of travertine (Italian limestone) slabs. The dark areas are actually open space, not stone: the walls are designed, said Kuma, so "the wind would sweep through." This detail achieves the effect of effortless suspension, drawing parallels between the lightness of the stone and the lotus petals. Born in 1956 in Yokohama, he rejects the idea of the city as a cultural and technological center, and the decline of the rural. Here, technology and nature come together in elegant harmony.

WALKER HOUSE, 1953
Sanibel Island, Florida, USA

PAUL RUDOLPH

This guesthouse exhibits a pure architectural ideal that is suited to its environment but not necessarily its site, a flat clearing of sand bounded by unkempt vegetation on Sanibel Island. Its timber structure was prefabricated because at the time of building, supplies could only reach the island by boat. Adhering to a cubic module, the pavilion is a compact 24 square feet (2.2 square meters). Inside, one half of the space is for living and dining; the other half contains a bedroom, bathroom, and kitchen. Offset exterior columns frame the structure and visually lighten an already nimble assembly. This frame supports a simple pulley system for opening plywood shutters on the house's four faces. When raised, a cannonball weight closes the shutters, and when lowered, it opens them up.

VILLA HEGARD, 1966

Oslo, Norway

JAN INGE HOVIG

Villa Hegard is one of only a few residential projects designed by the celebrated Norwegian architect Jan Inge Hovig. The strictly geometric structure of the villa features a series of cubical volumes, consecutively protruding to create a complex geometric layout with a rigid and heavy appearance. The central part is highlighted by a raw concrete surface and a vertical concrete grille, covering the windows of the living room and creating the vertical appearance of the structure. The adjacent lower wing has a cascading form of single rooms, offsetting each other. The main living room of the house features concrete surfaces and a wooden ceiling above the double-height space. A sloping glass roof, which is now part of the main structure, was added in 1990 by Kristian Biong Junior, who sensitively preserved the original ideas of Hovig.

POLITO HOUSE, 1938

Los Angeles, California, USA

RAPHAEL SORIANO

Within the Hollywood Hills, this Bauhaus-influenced house was designed for Anthony and Carmella Polito. The house is sleek and white, a three-story stuccoed cube created in the International Style. Its street-facing side is introverted, while the rear is more open with steel casement ribbon windows on the ground floor and a cutaway sun terrace. A bridge connects the third floor to an elevated garden on the facing slope. Soriano went on to design more informal structures, including a Case Study House (1950), in which he delighted in working with off-the-shelf materials, which fitted into a standardized grid system, the fundamental ordering principle behind all his work. Soriano began his career in the office of Richard Neutra, whose Lovell House (1929) was an early example of domestic steel construction.

VILLA ZAPU, 1984
Napa Valley, California, USA

POWELL-TUCK CONNOR
& OREFELT

The siting of the Villa Zapu, squarely on the prow of a hill, reflects the tradition of the villa in the manner of Palladio and Jefferson, while its specific form and details deconstruct and oppose its country house heritage. This duality takes on a different form in the interior, with the ground floor detailed and furnished in the manner of an eighteenth-century French château, while the first floor is in the style of 1930s Moderne. Designed in 1984 by the English architect David Connor, for a Californian client, the house duly reflects its schizophrenic nature. Similarly, the landscaping, by George Hargreaves, cleaves the line between nature and artifice by using a palette of indigenous plantings to create compelling but unnatural patterns. This modern-day manor created a sensation in the California wine country when it was first built.

HOUSE AT RIVA SAN VITALE, 1973

Ticino, Switzerland

MARIO BOTTA

The perilous-looking iron bridge emphasizes the isolation of this square-plan tower house, set on the hillside of Monte San Giorgio. Its pure form is typical of Botta's interest in "ideal" geometries, and he was one of a group of architects who looked back to the abstract forms of 1930s Italian Rationalism, seeking to create a contemporary monumentalism. Botta's work is often based on the simple forms of cube and cylinder found in ancient architecture, rather than on specific historical references. The bridge penetrates the tower and leads to a studio on the top floor, where stairs lead down to the other levels. The austere, steep site does not permit the luxury of a garden, but there is a porch on the lowest level which provides spectacular views over the snow-capped peaks above Lake Lugano.

THE RED HOUSE, 2002

Oslo, Norway

JARMUND/VIGSNÆS ARKITEKTER

In an area largely defined by postwar family housing, most of which are single dwellings rather than blocks, this building stands out as a beacon of vibrant color. The red exterior is typical of wood-clad houses in the Nordic region, and is particularly vivid against the snow. According to the architects, its red color is inspired by the client's temperament. Clinging to an incline above a river valley, the two-story house was built perpendicular to a nearby river to avoid blocking the sight lines of a house further uphill. The living spaces (and predominantly the areas for grownups) are on the upper level, with views toward the south and a covered west-facing terrace. Children's space is on the ground floor, with an outlook straight down to the river. This lookout aspect, and the separation between adults and kids, gives the house a sense of opportunities for fun.

OCEAN VIEW FARMHOUSE, 1995

Mount Nee, Queensland, Australia

ANDRESEN O'GORMAN ARCHITECTS

This farmhouse is sited just below the ridgeline, which ensures protection against the wind, but also opens the building to winter sun and wide views. It comprises a one-bedroom apartment with a string of attached service areas, including a laundry, workshops, and a tractor shed, and is defined by two primary walls. The south-facing wall, clad with metal sheets set vertically and overlaid with dark-stained timber battens, is seen on approach. The north wall is more permeable, and includes sliding doors and flyscreening. The house is seductively transparent at its extremities; the dining area, for example, has a corner screen of lead-light windows overlooking the coastline. The architects chose materials with colors derived from the landscape—a recurring feature in their work—in order for the house to have an easy relationship with its surroundings.

OBI-HOUSE, 2013

Bunkyo, Tokyo, Japan

TETSUSHI TOMINAGA
ARCHITECT & ASSOCIATES

This three-story building presents an enigmatic facade to a Tokyo street. The OBI-House appears enclosed and private, but the architects aspired to bring light and a limited sense of the outdoors in to the home in various clever ways. The street-facing facade features three stacked, white cuboid volumes that overlap, topped by a flat roof. Between each volume, there is a slender vertical aperture, which allows light to penetrate the house on each floor. Windows at the side and rear of the residence also illuminate and ventilate; some have small balconies decorated with greenery, creating outdoor space for the inhabitants. A small courtyard in the office area provides additional natural illumination, as do a series of light wells; and glass-and-wire-mesh flooring allows light to travel between floors.

VISITING ARTISTS HOUSE, 2003

Geyserville, California, USA

JIM JENNINGS ARCHITECTURE

This house is on the grounds of the Oliver Ranch, described by the curator Joan Simon as "an exquisite place and an extraordinary idea." Owned by Steve and Nancy Oliver, it is home to eighteen site-specific art installations, including works by Bill Fontana, Bruce Nauman, and Andy Goldsworthy. Disillusioned with the art business, the Olivers wanted to commission art that could be neither bought nor sold. This dwelling is a place to stay for visiting artists. Part house, part sculpture, it consists of two poured-in-place concrete walls—diverging to the north, converging to the south—containing a jewellike glass box. The inner walls are carved with a design by the Canadian visual artist David Rabinowitch; the house frames the landscape in extraordinary ways, more landscape intervention than building.

DESERT HOUSE, 2013
Alice Springs, Northern Territory, Australia

DUNN & HILLAM ARCHITECTS

Alice Springs is part of Australia's original outback, and the wider area is composed of multiple desert zones. In order to facilitate economy, Desert House was sited among layers of hard rock to take advantage of the earth's stable core temperature for cooling in the summer and warmth in winter. A slanted fly roof of corrugated steel cleverly shades a central courtyard that in turn sends cool air from the ground up for ventilation through floor-level windows. Warm air is released through roof vents to encourage the cycle. Its progressively sustainable program gives the Modernist house a Deconstructivist aesthetic. Solar evacuated tubes, CoolMax coating, and Photovoltaic arrays rarely get such overt placement; in this house, the display of functional resilience is elevated to have its own appeal.

TROUSDALE ESTATES, 1960s

Los Angeles, California, USA

A. QUINCY JONES & OTHERS

Developer Paul Trousdale had the vision to create an exclusive, leafy estate high above Los Angeles, in Beverly Hills, on a 410-acre (166-hectare) plot owned by the Doheny oil empire. Work began in 1954. The list of architects who designed projects here includes some of the best talent practicing at the time, including Allen Siple, Lloyd Wright (son of Frank Lloyd Wright), A. Quincy Jones, Wallace Neff, among others. An enclave sprang up in an eclectic range of styles, from California ranch to Hollywood Regency, Rustic Modern, organic, and International Style. Early residents included Groucho Marx and Barbara Stanwyck; in the 1960s, Elvis Presley, Dean Martin, and Richard Nixon also lived here. By the 1970s it was mocked as passé and nouveau riche, but more recently, due to a renewed interest in Modernism, it has enjoyed a renaissance.

AP HOUSE, 2017

Urbino, Italy

GGA GARDINI GIBERTINI ARCHITECTS

This development is a sensitive and imaginative re-creation of an ancient hamlet on one of the highest hills near Urbino in Marche. The new system of buildings reinterprets the traditional idiom of Marche architecture, and its layout is based on the plan of an old medieval settlement on the site. The AP House rests on a red concrete plinth, which also incorporates a swimming pool with wide views over the countryside. A main house is at the center of the arrangement, creating a dialog with the other volumes. Local stone was used for the simple, barnlike buildings, devoid of any extraneous ornament, and typical domestic elements, such as gutters or drainpipes. Wooden grille-like screens add a further classical geometry and rigor. The interior finishes and some furniture are custom-made by GGA using natural walnut wood.

GRAHAM HOUSE, 1962

West Vancouver, British Columbia, Canada

ARTHUR ERICKSON

The fluid dissolution of the distinction between manmade and natural—house and setting—is a trademark of Erickson's designs. Working at a time when Modern architecture was widely accepted, Erickson had the freedom to endow his works with a deep-seated appreciation for nature. This sensitivity characterized his seminal contribution to the creation of a North American "West Coast" architecture style. Here, hovering horizontal beams counterpointed the Graham House's incredibly steep site—a cliff face which drops 40 feet (12 meters) from the entry level down to a rock bench over the sea. The house, which featured wood throughout, with the exception of some Welsh quarry tile and brick, descended the slope in levels; on each level, a terrace opened onto the roof of the floor below. Sadly, it was demolished in 2007.

TARLO HOUSE, 1979

Sagaponack, New York, USA

TOD WILLIAMS ASSOCIATES

The Tarlo House is one of the most iconic houses of the 1970s. It responds not just to practical considerations but also to the site —a nondescript field—itself; it presents almost as a piece of land art. Yet it is never just pure sculpture, with each piece of the building formed and situated for functional reasons. Built for William Tarlo on a subdivided potato field near Wainscott, Long Island, a main orthogonal living block is orientated east–west to get the best views and through ventilation. On its north side is an enormous wooden screen offering privacy and wind protection, connecting to the house via a footbridge. On the south side, a brise-soleil shades the tall glazed facade. In such a featureless environment, the ensemble creates its own system of identity, which is rational, yet also totemic and strange.

MILLER HOUSE IN COLUMBUS, 1957

Columbus, Indiana, USA

EERO SAARINEN

Eero Saarinen, the son of Finnish architect Eliel Saarinen, already had a longtime familial connection with J. Irwin Miller when he was asked to design this house on the Flatrock River in Columbus. This classically modern home is actually four separate structures arranged into one unit. Inside, Saarinen used marble for walls and travertine for the floor, which extends outward onto an all-round veranda; the furnishings included rugs and chairs which Saarinen designed himself. The Millers commissioned two of only four built single-family residences by Saarinen, who is better known for his public buildings, including the T.W.A. Flight Center at Kennedy International Airport (1962). In this Columbus home, Saarinen used form in an abstract and symbolic manner quite different from the geometric form of the Miller Cottage in Ontario (1952).

TUGENDHAT HOUSE, 1930

Brno, Czech Republic

LUDWIG MIES VAN DER ROHE

Arguably Mies' finest European residence, the Tugendhat House is the archetypal Modern villa. Designed concurrently, the house is a domesticated version of the German Pavilion in Barcelona and utilizes the same stylistic concepts: a travertine floor, the use of luxurious materials such as chrome and onyx, and the cruciform steel column structure topped with a slab roof. The sloping site allowed for a revolutionary arrangement internally. The house is accessed from the top floor and the main living quarters are below, where uninterrupted glass walls face onto the garden. The flat roof, open-plan layout, and blank facade combined with innovative technologies make this a landmark building of early Modernism. However, while Modern design could be austerely functional, Mies uses high-quality finishes to endow this house with elegance.

WEIN HOUSE, 2014

Costa Esmeralda, Argentina

BESONÍAS ALMEIDA ARQUITECTOS

Used and enjoyed by two large families with small children as a holiday home, the Wein House stands on the top of a natural dune, surrounded by pine trees, establishing a perfect holiday location. The house is designed as a cascading structure of raw concrete, filled with expansive glass walls. The narrow ground plan includes a space for meetings of both families. The clients wanted to design a house with the possibility of expansion, and with large balconies to enjoy the view of the landscape. The ramp leading to the garage and to the entrance of the house is an important construction element that ensures the site is stable in sand. The house itself is composed of two main rectangular volumes which are tucked into the terrain, with a large terrace at the front and large overhanging concrete roofs.

REBBERG HOUSE, 1965

Zurich, Switzerland

HANS DEMARMELS

Rebberg House sits on a steep hillside overlooking Zurich, flanked by two other buildings in similar style, also by Demarmels, divided into two and three apartments, respectively. In the three-story architect's house, the design combines the horizontal and the vertical, recessed and projecting space into a harmonious whole. Occupying four split-level stories (children's rooms on the top floor, parents below, the living area on the ground floor, and studios in the basement), the interior layout centers on a hearth, around which wraps a concrete staircase. The various half-levels—seven in all—create a variety of spaces and nooks, making the most of the building's modest footprint. Few doors divide the interior: rooms flow seamlessly into one another, allowing glimpses from one space into the next.

TREE HOUSE, 1998

Cape Town, South Africa

VAN DER MERWE MISZEWSKI

The umbrella pines on the wooded slopes of Table Mountain near Cape Town suggested the conceptual design solution for this house. Five enormous tree-like structures anchor the roof, which sails over the spaces below. Underneath, the house relies on an ordering system of layers—starting with a masonry wall running the length of the house—to establish scale and privacy. Beyond this, a three-story void drops behind a secondary glass layer, allowing light into the deepest recesses of the house. Crossways, another series of layers and screens begins with the terrace opening up to the landscape, followed by the living room and, finally, bedrooms, bathrooms, and kitchens stacked at the rear. The project conveys the architects' preoccupation with bringing the house and its occupants into a dialog with nature.

ZERO COSMOLOGY, 1991

Kagoshima, Kyushu, Japan

MASAHARU TAKASAKI

The Zero Cosmology house is close to Sakurajima, a still-active volcano, and is made entirely of poured-in-place concrete. The house is squeezed onto a typical Japanese urban plot, and it is the living room that gives this house its name. It lies at the core of the building, with the more functional spine of rooms adjacent, and its importance as a place of refuge is symbolized by its ovoid shape—it is a space of security and privacy for the client. This room has various-sized holes punched through its concrete ceiling and achieves an interior that is midway between the simplicity of a Roman bath and the mystery of a modern-day planetarium. For Takasaki, organic architecture is not simply about putting people closer to nature through a building but it is also about introducing humans to a wider spiritual world.

CHALET, VAL D'HÉRENS, 2015

Saint-Martin, Switzerland

SAVIOZ FABRIZZI ARCHITECTES

The site of this chalet is a naturally occurring plateau near a mountain peak, which meant it could be constructed with minimal disruption to the terrain. Architects Savioz Fabrizzi designed it to benefit from the panoramic views—the valley and the Alps to the south and west, a village to the north and east—and its lines and forms are remarkably sharp. Outside, concrete is covered by wood cladding on the upper levels, referencing typical local chalets. The ground floor is in the form of a simple podium, overhung by the cantilevering second floor, which creates a shaded terrace. Inside, a central connecting concrete staircase links all four levels and creates a repeating visual element on each floor. Pale timber is used copiously on ceilings and walls as a warm material that contrasts with the lustrous polished concrete.

VAULT HOUSE, 2013

Oxnard, California, USA

JOHNSTON MARKLEE

On a densely developed site just north of Malibu, California, the Vault House largely rejects the standard beach-retreat typology— typically a big view of the ocean at the front with recessed, dimly lit rooms behind. Johnston Marklee designed the long, narrow volume, which is similar to the paradigm of a shotgun-house, as a series of vaulted spaces of varying heights, ensuring a continuous view from the street side to the beach side. A built-in courtyard at the center of the house means that every room has access to the outdoors. Perched on small stilts, the house achieves some unusual and beautiful forms. Its perspectives on the inside are compelling: one curving, shell-like space connects elegantly to the next. U-shaped cutouts add an interesting scalloped effect to the otherwise blank white facade.

GINAN HOUSE, 2012

Gifu, Gifu Prefecture, Japan

KEITARO MUTO ARCHITECTS

The beauty of Keitaro Muto's family garden inspired the main focus of Ginan House, which revolves around the placement of large garden stones brought from his parents' home. The house itself was approached conceptually as a "garden." Utilizing black gravel across much of the outdoor space gives the compound a sense of richness and fertility. The home, with its obliquely shaped walls and irregular, off-kilter volumes, resembles a growing organism which has been planted and nurtured. The two-story residence is separated between two buildings. The communal rooms are in the larger volume, while two bedrooms are in the smaller volume, which is accessible by an indoor footbridge. A pool is located outside, placed in a recessed area between the volumes that define the rear of the building.

RODE HOUSE, 2017

Chiloé Island, Chile

PEZO VON ELLRICHSHAUSEN

This house, sited above a ridge on the island of Chiloé, has an aura of mystery evoked by its unusual geometrical forms. Part of the Rode House is a sheltering crescent, which speaks of home, protection, and welcome. Both ends of the form sweep upward to create sharply pitching roofs. There is a bedroom in each of the volume's terminations, one facing north, the other south, experiencing diametrically opposite conditions of light and shade. Between them are living and dining areas. Native timber is used extensively inside and outside, and the house was constructed with the help of local craftspeople. Wood is reprised again on the shingle-clad roof, which dips as well as curves like the inside of a tire—inside, this translates to beautiful curves suggestive of the bow of a ship.

BLAIRGOWRIE HOUSE, 2012

Blairgowrie, Victoria, Australia

WOLVERIDGE ARCHITECTS

Thoughtful detailing makes this light, easygoing rendition of a beach house rise above the everyday. Commissioned by a couple with young children relocating to Port Phillip Bay, southern Australia, the house is wedged into a sand dune. To accommodate the difference in levels, one end of the house cantilevers outward, supported by stilts. Recycled wood is used on both exterior and interior cladding, while concrete and breezeblocks have also been incorporated into the building materials, making nostalgic reference to the archetypal Australian surfing clubhouse. The breezeblock motif is further picked up in laser-cut screening which shelters an inner courtyard, casting geometric shadows on the timber walls of the house. A row of stelae, made of rammed earth, lead a path through the garden to the entrance.

CUBE HOUSE, 2008

Sesto, Italy

PLASMA STUDIO

Wedged between two more traditionally designed neighbors, this faceted dwelling is located in Sesto, high among the Dolomite mountains. The steepness of the plot—and the limited space available—dictated the form of the house. Cooking, eating, and living areas are arranged tightly on the first floor around a central staircase, while bedrooms are on the second floor. Cantilevering terraces, however, provide additional space outdoors. Wooden slats are used as facade screening to protect privacy, occasionally opening up to reveal the beauty of the mountain views around the house. Triangular sections of the facade appear to have been "unfolded" from the building and joined to the ground, so there is no clear transition between house and earth. From the rear, the building is rendered white, like other vernacular houses nearby.

SUNNYLANDS, 1966
Palm Springs, California, USA

A. QUINCY JONES

For more than forty years, Walter and Leonore Annenberg hosted and entertained high-profile meetings at this most unusual of Californian estates. Walter was a newspaper tycoon, philanthropist, and ambassador to the UK; he and Leonore welcomed presidents, the British royal family, and other rich and famous guests. Bucking the American trend for historical pastiche winter residences, Sunnylands was a career highlight for Jones, who designed perhaps the most purely Modernist estate in America, which included eleven fishing lakes and a golf course with a totem pole. The typical midcentury Modern house is raised up on terraces surrounded by pink sloping concrete walls alluding to Mayan architecture. The statement roof, a motif in Jones's work, is also pink—to echo sunrises and sunsets on the nearby mountains—at the suggestion of Leonore.

VILLA SPIES, 1969

Torö, Sweden

STAFFAN BERGLUND

Rising like an elegant hemispherical spacecraft above the rocky coastline, the Villa Spies is a summer house designed by Staffan Berglund for the wealthy Danish business genius Simon Spies. The villa's futuristic features include a circular dining space, which rises out of the ground at the press of a button, sound-proofed walls, electric shutters, electronically controlled lighting, and a heated outdoor swimming pool. With a band of windows in place of an outer wall, the house has a 360-degree view to the sea. Spies originally founded his business on tourism and set up a competition in 1967 to design an environment for leisure in the country which both visitors and residents could enjoy. Although Berglund's original entry won the "Bubbles for Pleasure" competition, it was never built; however, his ideas inspired Spies to commission this villa.

YAKISUGI HOUSE, 2007

Nagano, Nagano Prefecture, Japan

TERUNOBU FUJIMORI

The Yakisugo House in Nagano was inspired by a trip that architect Terunobu Fujimori took to a small cave dwelling near Lascaux in France. The cave informed the primeval feel of the building, the shape of the entrance to the house—a truncated hexagon—and the living area and kitchen with sloping ceilings. These zones give the sense of being enclosed and safe in a warm, wood-clad space. The structure's form is distinctive for its boxlike turret, which houses a tea room and tops one end of the house; from here, the roof pitches steepiy to create a wedge shape. The extremes of high and low create a playful tension in the building. It is clad in 26-foot (8-meter) lengths of charred cedar, which was warped during construction. The gaps were filled in with plaster, which gives the house an op art look.

T-HOUSE, 1992

Wilton, New York, USA

SIMON UNGERS &
THOMAS KINSLOW

The dominant T-shape of this house contains both residential accommodation and a workspace and library for its owner. The two stories of the bar of the T are divided horizontally into solid and void. The solid top half houses the stacks of books on a mezzanine and the transparent lower half, with views out to the woods, is for working and reading. Visitors enter the house across a promenade deck above the residential part of the house, a low-slung pavilion that emerges from the slope of the site—the only external clue to the presence of which is a funnel-like chimney. The dramatic orange color of the cladding comes from the effect of the weathering steel shell, which is further dramatized by the regular spacing of black, vertical glazed slots. It is an abstract composition, difficult to read without any sense of scale.

CASA CORINNA, 1963

Ticino, Switzerland

PEPPO BRIVIO

For this family home positioned on a hill above Breggia in Ticino, Peppo Brivio took advantage of the sloping site. His plan responds to the topography, being arranged over two levels, with the lower floor for bedrooms and bathing partially set into the hillside. This created a broad horizontal platform for the living and dining floor above. The commission also allowed Brivio to explore his idea of the modern facade further, creating a series of spaces he described as enjoying "liberation in height." The modular compositon of Casa Corinna enjoys an envelope shaped by orthogonal planes offset from each other and arranged in vertical and horizontal sequences. The effect is at once substantial and airy: the breaks between blocks introduce natural light into interiors. At the same time, voids are strategically positioned to maximize views across the plains.

WHITE U HOUSE, 1976

Nakano, Tokyo, Japan

TOYO ITO

This house consists of a continuous U-shaped volume with an inward-sloping roof and a rectangular volume connecting its two ends. The continuous interior space contains a minimal number of enclosed rooms. Ito intended the house's interior to be a fluid zone where light distribution, air movement, and human activities would be perceived as in flow. In addition, he experimentally arranged the elements in the curved area—including skylights, fluorescent cove lights, and furniture—with their own corresponding curves. The phenomenological experience that this generated was meant to express a physical sense of rhythm that the inhabitants might exhibit during the course of daily living. Ito's design demonstrated that a house can significantly affect human experience and, at the same time, it challenged conventional designs for a dwelling.

PLOCEK HOUSE, 1977

Warren, New Jersey, USA

MICHAEL GRAVES

From its sloping wooded site, the Plocek House projects a classical street-side facade, its three stories divided into basement, *piano nobile*, and attic. The house boasts a grand entrance intended both to reinforce its sense of scale and to imbue it with human proportions. A garden pavilion, set apart from the house, serves as a quiet study. With its reinterpreted, exaggerated classicism and muted palette, the Plocek House was the first of Graves's buildings to show this development in his style. Originally influenced by the Modernism of Le Corbusier, Graves became one of the New York Five architects, and was also a member of the Memphis Group, and a leader of the postmodern movement. He moved toward designing witty and erudite buildings that had a human scale and exaggerated historical forms.

JELLYFISH HOUSE, 2013

Marbella, Spain

WIEL ARETS ARCHITECTS

The pièce de résistance of this Mediterranean home is a huge glass-bottomed pool that cantilevers 30 feet (9 meters) out from the top floor—a quite exceptional technical accomplishment for a house of modest size. When planning, the architects knew neighboring houses would block the proposed home's view of the sea; raising the pool and sundeck solved the problem. The pool has a panoramic window at its interior-facing edge, meaning that those in the kitchen can watch swimmers as they glide about. Light shines through the glass bottom and walls of the pool to cast turquoise shimmers on the terrace below. Built of white poured-in-place concrete, the house assumes a form that resembles a giant waterborne creature. The interiors are characterized by polished concrete and glazed surfaces, which take on a light green tint.

GUNNLØGSSON HOUSE, 1958

Rungsted Strandvej, Denmark

HALLDOR GUNNLØGSSON

One of the protagonists of the "new tradition" in post-war Danish architecture, Gunnløgsson imbued this house with his interpretation of a traditional Danish lifestyle. The house acknowledges the impact on Danish architecture of such influential figures as Mies van der Rohe and Frank Lloyd Wright. This can be observed in the rigorous modular plan and the simple load-bearing timber structure with brick infill. In contrast to these influences, Gunnløgsson incorporated more traditional elements, such as a central fireplace and fir-board ceilings. Furniture and fittings are designed by some of his well-known countrymen, such as Poul Kjaerholm and Arne Jacobsen, and complement the open spatial quality of the house. With its simple, open plan and finely detailed traditional timber, stone, and brick, the house constitutes one of the finest Modern houses built in Denmark.

GREENWOOD HOUSE, 1951

Pretoria, South Africa

NORMAN EATON

Rough stone and materials that look as if they have come from their surroundings were characteristic of Eaton's work. The carefully contrived siting, the corner window in the dining room, and stone and timber finishes all show an affinity with the Arts and Crafts movement which had influenced Eaton while traveling in Europe in the early 1930s. Meanwhile, several close contemporaries strove to make Modernism acceptable in South Africa—a quest boosted by the arrival of several refugees from Nazi Germany. Eaton's houses, however, developed a consciously African architecture, using local materials and skills, for instance in decorative paving. The servants' quarters in this house—the art of planning for domestic staff lasted longer in South Africa than elsewhere—are an extraordinary composition of round forms and thatched roofs.

HAUS FEURER, 1992

St Anna am Aigen, Austria

WOLFGANG FEYFERLIK

The almost traditional farmhouse roof of the Haus Feurer dissolves, as if by magic or time, to bring a dappled light inside. Glass tiles provide a view upward, and thus a relationship to the sky, while the arrangement of the rooms affords views in all directions. The connection of the house to its site is also made explicit in the kitchen, which sits 17 inches (45 centimeters) below ground level to give the feeling of being part of the landscape. The house is built around a U-shaped courtyard, its three concrete frames ascending in size as they step around. The house is typical of the architect's design approach in its simple spaces, which are made special by their proportion and transparency to the outside. Feyferlik is one of several Graz architects who evolved a new Austrian avant-garde, displacing and reusing modern and traditional forms.

BENTLEY WOOD, 1938

Halland, England, UK

SERGE IVAN CHERMAYEFF

This two-story, long-fronted house stands in a broad landscape, stretching out an arm to one side where, as if held in the hand, a majestic stone carving by Henry Moore surveys the distant scene. Completed shortly before World War II, Bentley Wood was recognized as the most mature of English Modern houses of the 1930s. Chermayeff integrated its white-painted, timber-frame structure and cladding with its grid-like visual form, using timber unsentimentally, as if it were steel. The plan, a model for relaxed weekend living, was designed for the architect and his family. Frank Lloyd Wright visited in 1939, remarking, "It'll take a little time for God to make it click," but contemporary critics recognized Bentley Wood's aristocratic poise and the effortless convergence of modern ideas of space with older themes in landscape design.

STEINER HOUSE, 1910

Vienna, Austria

ADOLF LOOS

The curved metal roofline of the street front of this house masks its scale and the fact that it is built on three levels; more importantly, that the rear facade is rectilinear and flat-roofed, evidence of Loos's perception of architecture as spatial sequences, or Raumplan. One of the first houses to be constructed of reinforced concrete, the Steiner House is also one of few built works by Loos, a famous polemicist against the elaborate decoration of the Art Nouveau and Vienna Secessionist movements. Apart from the curved roof, the geometric form and rear garden facade of the house anticipate later Modern characteristics, such as functional interior spaces, solid white cubic forms, and horizontal fenestration. Loos, influenced by Louis Sullivan's work, fought against ornamentation; his famous essay "Ornament and Crime" was published in 1908.

VILLA RONCONI, 1973

Rome, Italy

SAVERIO BUSIRI VICI

Saverio Busiri Vici's layering of exposed concrete planes became a characteristic design motif. After several early, modest buildings, he grew increasingly experimental in his approach to concrete as a material to shape building forms. The house occupies a corner site in a residential neighborhood and its design includes facades of fairfaced concrete with geometric layered planes that step in and out around the perimeter. The tiered surfaces created from bold cantilevered planes and deep recesses produce dramatic patterns of shadow and light. Organized over two levels, the stout L-shaped plan hinges about a central stairwell with interlocking square volumes set around this core. Walls and windows step in and out around the periphery. Perhaps as a nod to the pitched-roof homes nearby, the project is crowned by a raked roof split in two.

K VALLEY HOUSE, 2015

Thames, New Zealand

HERBST ARCHITECTS

Named for its location in the Kauaeranga Valley, a verdant, deep river gorge ninety minutes from Auckland, this house was built as a haven between location shoots for a couple working in the film industry. A simple rectangular volume, straddling the ridgeline, contains the open-plan, double-height residence, engaged with the slope at the high end and floating above the land as it drops away. The house is surrounded on three sides by glazing, granting panoramic views of the valley. Recycled materials—wood and corroded corrugated iron sheets—were gathered by the client and incorporated into the building, creating a vernacular aesthetic and working in harmony with the colors of the landscape—a rural camouflage of sorts. The design also includes a small farm that allows the clients to have a self-sufficient lifestyle.

ST ANDREWS BEACH HOUSE, 1991

Mornington Peninsula, Victoria, Australia

NONDA KATSALIDIS

More like a beached shipping container than a home, St Andrews Beach House, said its architect, is a fusion of sentimental vernacular sources with the abstract traditions at the heart of Modernism. The house's rusty-looking, Corten steel and rough-hewn wood planking are reminiscent of traditional Australian building forms— the sort of rough-and-ready barns and outbuildings that you find in small settlements up and down the country. Yet here, Katsalidis has put them together with such knowing precision that they take on quite different connotations. The house has a straightforward arrangement: the heavy sections of recycled timber provide privacy for the bedroom wing; the living space is a large double-height area, glazed at ground-floor level, and clad above in Corten steel, the russet color of which is echoed in the surrounding vegetation.

A HOUSE FOR ESSEX, 2015

Essex, England, UK

FAT & GRAYSON PERRY

Overlooking the scenic Stour Estuary is this eccentric house, commissioned by philosopher and critic Alain de Botton's Living Architecture program: it is artist Grayson Perry's "chapel," which enshrines and celebrates the history of Essex, his home county. The chapel's architecture is inspired by Russian stave churches; the exterior is decorated with around two thousand tiles; and the golden roof is topped with sculptures, all designed by Perry. The window size increases from front to back, "growing" with the downward slope of the hill. A double-height central living area is adorned with Perry's intricate tapestries and ceramic works, and rooms have bold color schemes. A set of steps leads from the back of the house across a threshold decorated with a mosaic skull pattern onto a stretch of lawn. Visitors can apply to stay by ballot.

48 STOREY'S WAY, 1913

Cambridge, England, UK

MACKAY HUGH BAILLIE SCOTT

Sweeping roofs, shingle-hung gables, asymmetrical composition, and traditional, economical materials (such as roughcast render) give this home its verncular feel. Inside, the sitting room, with its low ceilings, timber beams, and inglenook, has a medieval feel, but two details place it firmly in the twentieth century—the innovative free-flowing space and considered use of materials. It is a complex room that manages to combine formal axial routes (between the dining and sitting rooms, and the front and garden doors), large gathering areas, and small intimate spaces, all with deceptive ease. In true Arts and Crafts tradition, materials are finished according to their use. This is one of the many individual house commissions that Baillie Scott undertook, but his housing schemes, such as Waterlow Court (1909), set new standards in house planning.

HOUSE IN OLD WESTBURY, 1971

Old Westbury, New York, USA

RICHARD MEIER

"Whiteness is one of the characteristic qualities of my work; I use it to clarify architectural concepts and heighten the power of visual form," Meier has said. The visual—and spatial—power of this Long Island mansion, both inside and out, is undeniable. Built for a family with six children, it had to accommodate multiple bedrooms and bathrooms and includes a library, a gallery hall with curving skylights, an office, and an art studio. Private areas are arranged in a linear formation facing a grove, while public spaces are free-flowing and overlook a lawn with lake. Meier employed his usual trademarks: complex facades that are a medley of projecting and recessing spaces; nautically styled balcony rails; striking columns; dramatic interior ramps; and, naturally, brilliant white walls, inside and out.

STAMP HOUSE, 2013

Cape Tribulation, Queensland, Australia

CHARLES WRIGHT ARCHITECTS

Cape Tribulation in northern Queensland has a tropical climate prone to cyclones. Set within the delicate environment of the Daintree Rainforest, the Stamp House consists of six low-slung concrete pods that cantilever far out over a lake. The house is designed to withstand extremes of heat, wind, and rain. The client for whom the project was originally built was a philatelic dealer, and the house's concrete facades do feature a pattern suggesting the perforated edges of postage stamps. But it is also known as "Alkira," which means the "Sky." Unwalled communal spaces are completely open to natural ventilation and provide plenty of shade from the fierce sun. Charles Wright said the client "didn't have much of a brief, he just said 'give me something that will blow my mind.'" That, ultimately, is exactly what the architect did.

RED CROSS HOUSE, 1991

Islamorada, Florida, USA

JERSEY DEVIL

At the core of this rugged and experimental house in the Florida Keys is a little block-and-stucco cottage, one of dozens erected by the Red Cross in 1935 after a destructive hurricane swept through Florida. The architects, Jersey Devil—so named as they established their practice in the state of New Jersey—are nomadic, moving from site to site in their Airstream trailer, settling in for the duration of the project's construction. With the cottage as their starting point, they created a complex construction that provides accommodation for family living and work space. Using commonplace materials, the building was assembled so as to withstand the sometimes fierce tropical weather—in particular hurricanes. The result is a study in corrugated steel and glass: a house that affords long views out to the ocean and across the middle Keys from its tower lookout.

HOUSE IN HAMADAYAMA, 2006

Suginami, Tokyo, Japan

SATOSHI OKADA

Land in Tokyo is in high demand, and plots can be tiny. From this challenge has emerged the city's trend of *jutaku*—fantastically creative microhouses responding to the shortage of space. Resembling a metal filing cabinet, this house is a tall, 753-square-foot (70-square-meter) box. It is actually built with a wooden structure, where spaces overlap one another with a half-story shift. The timber elements are supported by an eastern load-bearing wall. The minimal window slits at the front facade are compensated for with larger openings at the rear, and zenithal light flows into the building through the central stairwell. On each floor there is a single room, while the bathroom cantilevers out from the first floor. In the context of the Tokyo streetscape, a louvered metal skin gives the house a lustrous aesthetic.

HEMMELIG ROM, 2015

Ellenville, New York, USA

STUDIO PADRON

Architecture at this scale delights for its ability to have an impact despite its diminutive size. "Hemmelig Rom," which means "Secret Library" in Norwegian, is a tiny guesthouse for photographer Jason Koxvold's vacation home in upstate New York. The single-room hut, sited in pine woods, was built by hand from mature oak trees which were felled during the building of the main house, recycling what would have been construction waste. Cut, shaped, and allowed to dry over several years, the logs were then layered horizontally, similarly to Jenga blocks, to create interior walls with bespoke nooks for storing more than one thousand books. The volume is also a heatsink, storing energy from the single cast-iron stove. The external cladding is black wood; during the winter, the inky cube provides a striking visual contrast to the snow.

GAMBLE HOUSE, 1908

Pasadena, California, USA

GREENE & GREENE

One of the Greene brothers' "ultimate bungalows," the Gamble House exhibits the plaited nature and superb craftsmanship of their aesthetic: an interweaving of textures, of timber shingles, clinker brick, and wooden battening. The layered nature of this construction also reflects an interweaving of traditions: Gustav Stickley and the American Arts and Crafts movement, and the Japanese tradition of wooden construction were synthesized in a vernacular regionalist idiom shared by such other California architects as Bernard Maybeck and Julia Morgan. The house is less open on the interior than Frank Lloyd Wright's Prairie houses, but makes extensive use of verandas to exploit views. Rich interiors of mahogany and teakwood exude a sense of ease suitable to the relaxed lifestyle of Pasadena at the turn of the century.

VILLA SAVOYE, 1931

Poissy, France

LE CORBUSIER

The Villa Savoye is an icon of functionalist, machine-age symbolism, embodying many of Le Corbusier's revolutionary concepts, such as the "Five Points of a New Architecture." The use of the slender columns, pilotis, to support the main living area above the ground gives the house a striking elegance, while the thin strip windows on all sides unify the design. Made possible by the development of reinforced concrete technology, the pilotis enabled Le Corbusier to separate stationary living space from a ground zone given over to moving objects, or traffic. Inside, a ramp leads from ground level up toward the rooftop solarium, dramatizing a sense of movement through the house. This house is an eloquent expression of Le Corbusier's influential vision of a rationalized architecture, which would lift its inhabitants into a realm of light, air, and order.

ROSE SEIDLER HOUSE, 1950

Sydney, New South Wales, Australia

HARRY SEIDLER

Graduating from Harvard University in 1946, where he was taught by ex-Bauhaus members Walter Gropius and Marcel Breuer, Seidler left for Australia to design a house in Sydney for his parents. The Rose Seidler House was the first building of a prolific career, which spanned more than fifty years and ranged from small domestic projects to high-rise apartments and office towers. A hollowed-out, floating white box, the house is anchored to the ground by a series of elements that extend from the main volume, such as the garden retaining walls and the visually dominant ramp. The open terrace, with its mural painted by Seidler, links the living and bedroom spaces. In 1988, the Historic Houses Trust opened the house to the public, reinforcing its status as an important work of Modernism and one of the most influential houses in Australia.

HAUS IN MOOSBURG, 1996

Moosburg, Germany

SZYSZKOWITZ-KOWALSKI

Within a softly undulating Bavarian landscape, this eccentric house hugs the slope of a green hillside. On a longitudinal plan, it is built over two levels, which step downhill. Its arcing roof sweeps over the house to contain and protect it. At the introverted street-facing side, where visitors enter, it has a deep overhang; on the valley side, it opens up but is extended by elegantly curving gutters, which turn it into one seamless piece of sculpture. These carry rainwater off to a small underground pond. With its concrete and double-height glazing, the valley-facing facade is loftily imposing, almost ecclesiastical. Color plays an important role in the design: bright fins on the roof add quirky detail. Since the 1970s Graz-based Szyszkowitz-Kowalski has developed an architectural approach that engages residents and passersby in an emotional way.

GELLER HOUSE II, 1969

Long Island, New York, USA

MARCEL BREUER

When the Gellers, for whom Breuer had designed the first important house of his independent practice, approached him to design a second house, he suggested that they employ a variation of his unbuilt design for the Paepcke vacation house (1959) in Aspen, Colorado. In that design, Breuer had proposed a form strikingly different from his typical domestic designs: a long, low arcing vault of concrete. In this project, the elevation facing the marsh and ocean views is fully glazed and has a dynamic composition of intersecting horizontal and non-aligned vertical concrete planes. Inside, a studio on the mezzanine level, which has a sauna and bathroom, is set beneath the arcing ceiling and overlooks the main open-plan living space below. Bedrooms are arranged to the north, and face the shallow entry court.

VILLA MAIREA, 1939

Noormarkku, Finland

ALVAR & AINO AALTO

The Villa Mairea, to be used as a summer house, was intended to express the clients Harry and Maire Gullichsen's vision of modern life. It is also a decisive shift from functionalism to a more organic Modernism for Alvar Aalto. With his wife, Aino, undertaking the interior design, the couple used this project as a test bed for a mix of new formal concepts, synthesizing into what Alvar labeled a "flexible" order; in contrast with conventional Modernist practice, Aalto did everything he could to avoid what he called "artificial architectural rhythms in the building." The villa was intended to evoke the experience of being in a forest, through a collage of textures—rattan-wrapped supporting columns, treelike poles that screen the staircase, teak and stone cladding, grass roofs—and seamless transitioning from outside to inside.

AV HOUSE, 2011

Mar Azul, Argentina

BAKARQUITECTOS

BAKarquitectos, which comprised Argentinian architects María Victoria Besonías and Guillermo de Almeida, designed this weekend home at the heart of a forest on a gently sloping plot in Mar Azul, a coastal town in Buenos Aires Province. The two-bedroom house is formed of four connecting orthogonal volumes, which gradually descend the slope on an east–west axis. The board-formed concrete references the organic forms of the woods around the house and will weather over time, further integrating the building to the site; its horizontality also forms a counterpoint to the verticality of the trees. The simple material scheme includes openings formed of dark bronze anodized aluminum. Glazing is generous on the north facade to capture as much sunlight as possible. Apart from the sofas, beds, and chairs, all of the built-in furniture is made of concrete.

CASA GASPAR, 1992

Cádiz, Spain

ALBERTO CAMPO BAEZA

The work of Campo Baeza stands out for the ingenuity of his geometric volumes. The high exterior walls of Casa Gaspar form a perfect square, and are unfenestrated despite its pretty setting in an orange grove in southern Spain. The introspective plan is split into three equal parts—two courtyards on either side of the central house—all of which emphasize a control of direct and reflected light. The relationship between the interior and the patio is crucial to the success of the house, and Campo Baeza emphasizes the link through a series of devices such as the apparent continuation of materials. Although the white planar architecture recalls the Purist movement of the early twentieth century, the house's simple plan and stark geometry are indebted to Mies van der Rohe's courtyard house studies of the 1930s, as well as to the work of Luis Barragán.

MERZ HOUSE, 1959

Môtiers, Switzerland

ATELIER 5

Beneath the pervasive vines that cover this house lies a concrete structure, built as a solitary object in the tradition of Le Corbusier. It was designed by a group of Swiss architects who self-consciously continued exploring the formal language of their architectural mentor and fellow countryman in the post-war period. The two-story house, with large picture windows facing onto a lake, rests on pilotis and is contained within a governing frame. The living, dining, kitchen, and bedroom areas are on the raised first floor, with a guest room and sun terrace on the second floor. Since its inception in 1955, Atelier 5 has strived toward achieving an "anonymous architecture" in a truly mutual, collaborative process, with housing as a theme and central mission, and is best known for its Halen housing estate near Berne (1955–60).

GREENE RESIDENCE, 1961

Norman, Oklahoma, USA

HERB GREENE

Herb Greene based the form of his own house on that of the American buffalo, which used to roam the prairies of the Midwest. He tried to inject a feeling of pathos into the "looming, wounded creature" that is the house; but it also evokes a natural shelter, with the entrance under a metaphorical spreading wing, like that of a mother hen. There is a sense of accretion and collage, an organic gathering of form and materials to create a strong physical presence. Inside, the house is cave-like, the irregularly layered wooden shingles creating a comforting texture, while the relation of the different levels and the expression of the exterior form internally are both vertiginous and dramatic. Greene studied under Bruce Goff, whose expressionistic and eclectic style clearly influenced Greene's work, as well as his humanistic approach to organic architecture.

BORDEAUX-LE PECQ HOUSE, 1966

Bois-le-Roi, France

CLAUDE PARENT

The country house of painter and art collector Andrée Bordeaux-Le Pecq sits on a hillside in Bois-le-Roi, Normandy. This domestic setting gave Claude Parent an opportunity to investigate his architectural theory of the "oblique function" at a more intimate scale. Through this approach, Parent sought to advocate "the death of the vertical line as an axis for elevation[s]." At Bois-le-Roi, the roofs provide the main expression of his resistance against Cartesian architectural compositions. This resistance is not only seen in their angled pitches but also in the three-part floor plan, which responds in orientation and scale to the varied roof spans. As a counterpoint to the dominant concrete roofs, the majority of the project is clad with full-height glazing or sliding doors and its internal arrangement is largely open-planned.

MEDHURST HOUSE, 2008

Medhurst, Victoria, Australia

DENTON CORKER MARSHALL

Medhurst House is set above rolling vineyards in Victoria's Yarra Valley. The house is characterized by two identical "black horizontal strokes" that form the floor and roof plate—the black underside of which accentuates the bold presence of the building in the landscape. A series of hefty black-pigmented concrete-blade walls, staggered perpendicular to the plates, form the base, at one end retaining the hillside. A dramatic cantilever shelters a paved terrace at the opposing end. The lower level accommodates car parking, a wine cellar, bedrooms, and a study. The wide stairway in the entry foyer leads to the upper level, which contains living and bedroom spaces. Views through the opposite facade are controlled through horizontal slit windows in the two distinctive green bands stretched across the elevation.

ROBIE HOUSE, 1910
Chicago, Illinois, USA

FRANK LLOYD WRIGHT

The Robie House is a consummate expression of Wright's Prairie Style, which the architect developed to suit the big, open landscapes of the American Midwest. Regarded as the first truly American architectural idiom, it used low, horizontal volumes; natural materials such as brick, wood, and limestone; cantilevered roofs; and long bands of stained-glass windows; and the interior and exterior were conceived to be totally integrated. The client, businessman Frederick C. Robie, requested as modern a home as possible. Wright's design was revolutionary, not least in having burglar alarms, a central vacuum system, and a connected garage. After a change in fortune, Robie had to sell the house a year after completion. It has been used as a classroom, dormitory, refectory, and office but is now open to the public for tours.

WILEY HOUSE, 1953

New Canaan, Connecticut, USA

PHILIP JOHNSON

Philip Johnson designed several Modern homes in New Canaan, including the Glass House (1949). This is arguably his most ambitious. Nestled into a grassy site surrounded by forest, this structure consists of a rectangular stone base, containing bedrooms and bathrooms, topped by a double-height glass-and-wood structure, intersecting at ninety degrees, which comprises a kitchen and living areas. Designed for real-estate developer Robert Wiley, the T-shaped plan creates space for a large porch and enables the glass portion to cantilever over its solid base. The gently sloping property also contains a barnlike, metal-clad art gallery designed by Roger Ferris + Partners, as well as Johnson's original circular pool and "lily pad" diving platform. The home, shaded by curved awnings, is supported by a grid of glass panels.

HOUSE AT MARTHA'S VINEYARD, 1988

Martha's Vineyard, Massachusetts, USA

STEVEN HOLL

This spare structure was created as a two-bedroom vacation house at Martha's Vineyard. Inspired by a passage in Herman Melville's *Moby-Dick*, in which a sailor recounts a Native American practice of making a shelter from a beached whale carcass, Holl employed the wooden balloon-frame structure as an exoskeleton, exposed on two of the four sides of the house as a veranda. The cubic volume, clad in horizontal wood boards and topped by a conning towerlike lookout, firmly anchors the house to its hilltop site. The elongated home steps down in five sections, following the gentle fall of the land, while the roof remains flat. A projecting, V-shaped glazed dining room, along with the tower, protrude from the main, containerlike body. By 2014 the poetic, imposing structure was riddled with dry rot, and it was demolished.

PRICE HOUSE, 1989

Corona del Mar, California, USA

BART PRINCE

A shimmering swimming pool is at the heart of the living core of this spectacularly creative ocean-front home. Three structurally autonomous timber pods connect to create a fantastical composition full of hidden rooms, in some ways recalling a Japanese teahouse. The wooden shingle cladding, traditionally associated with the seaside, is here taken to a new level. Following his mentor, Bruce Goff, Prince refuses to fall into any of the conventional categories of architecture. He works closely with his clients and his projects are often constructed with a variety of materials, textures, and colors that reflect his interest in organic forms. The client for this house, Joe Price, is well known among architects for convincing his father to commission Frank Lloyd Wright to design the Price Tower in Bartlesville, Oklahoma in 1956.

CANOAS HOUSE, 1953

Rio de Janeiro, Brazil

OSCAR NIEMEYER

The curving roofline is the intuitive gesture that sets the organic organization for Niemeyer's own house, whose fluid spaces revolve around a natural boulder. The house's unassuming nature and embracing patio confirm Niemeyer as a man whose humility is born of his love for his native country. While influenced by Le Corbusier, with whom he worked early in his career, Niemeyer nonetheless continues to draw his primary inspiration from the spirit and imagery of Brazil. "The straight line, hard, inflexible, created by man, does not attract me," he wrote. "What does draw me is the free and sensual curve … The curve I find in the mountains of my country, in the clouds of the sky, and the waves of the sea." This plasticity inspires Niemeyer even in his large-scale projects, such as the many public buildings of the new city of Brasilia (1957–60).

VORONOI'S CORRALS, 2012

Milos, Greece

DECA ARCHITECTURE

Sited on a nature estate on the Greek island of Milos, Voronoi's Corrals is a house with a primitive quality. The architects selected points in different microenvironments within the site that were representive of various geologies, sun trajectory, flora, views, and audibility of the sea. These points were then used to generate a simple grid, based on the ideas of Russian mathematician Georgy Voronoi, which informed the geometry of the main house. The house is built from limestone blocks, which form a gleaming white canopy. Similar to a primordial shell, the roof slants downward from a central keystone, diminishing the mass of the roofline and anchoring a courtyard in the center of the rooms. The house's direct engagement with surrounding vegetation and the sea blurs the threshold between an indoor and outdoor life.

VIEIRA DE CASTRO HOUSE, 1994

Vila Nova de Famalicão, Portugal

ÁLVARO SIZA

This project is sited 11 miles (18 kilometers) south of Braga, high up on a hillside abundant with oak and pine. It commands spectacular views of the village of Vila Nova de Famalicão and the plain which surrounds it, and sensitively intrudes into the site. The two-story structure is formed of intersecting volumes, providing it with a geometric clarity that is typical of Siza's work. Inside, flooring, door frames, and wall paneling are made of natural wood, in contrast with the bright white decor. Voids create light-filled galleried spaces, while minimalist loggia encourage a sense of the outdoors being brought in, and maximize opportunities to take in the views. Siza, who was awarded the Pritzker Prize in 1992, originally wanted to be a sculptor; the plastic beauty of his buildings has been classified as poetic Modernism.

POLE PASS RETREAT, 2013

San Juan Islands, Washington, USA

OLSON KUNDIG

There are 172 named islands in the San Juan archipelago. This idyllic retreat occupies one of these, on a densely wooded plot facing out toward the Salish Sea. To take advantage of the island's pure air and temperate climate, the house needed to be as flexible as possible for inside and outside living. On the low-slung, two-story pavilion, a massive sedum roof cantilevers outward, covering the deck. Thanks to a system of gears and chains cranked by a hand-turned wheel, the pavilion's glass walls—the largest of which is 20 feet (6 meters) long—can be slid back completely. The interior and exterior further become one and the same in details such as a cantilevered kitchen counter, which extends to the outdoors. Cedarwood cladding was utilized, slightly charred in a Japanese weatherproofing technique called *shou sugi ban*.

GOULDING HOUSE, 1972

Enniskerry, Ireland

SCOTT TALLON WALKER

Jutting out over the River Dargle, Ronald Tallon's Goulding House might seem more suited to the hills of Los Angeles than the rural backwater of Enniskerry in Ireland. This extraordinary summerhouse was built for Sir Basil and Lady Goulding, who wanted a place in their back garden to hold parties and conferences. Tallon, of Dublin architects Scott Tallon Walker, came up with a Mies-influenced single-story design, which is just 33 feet (10 meters) long. Two bays of the steel-framed structure, diagonally braced on the exterior, are anchored to the hillside, while the remaining three cantilever out over the river. Two are completely glazed, the rest clad in cedar, which softens the otherwise crisp, High-Tech styling. Scott Tallon Walker was better known for its larger industrial and public buildings, including Caroll's Factory in Dundalk (1973).

CHICAGO HOUSE, 1998
Chicago, Illinois, USA

TADAO ANDO ARCHITECT
& ASSOCIATES

Although Ando, the Japanese minimalist master of sublime concrete structures, may be best known for building museums, galleries, and churches, he captured the same contemplative atmosphere of his institutional projects in this private house, one of his first buildings in the United States. The house is composed of two wings joined on the ground floor by a vast living and dining room and upstairs by an outdoor terrace reached either by indoor stairs or by an exterior ramp outside the living room. The concrete ramp rises out of a shallow reflecting pool—a favorite motif in Ando's work—separating the two wings of the house. At first blush, the house might appear large and impersonal, but it soon becomes clear that the architect designed a very private home with an added layer of atmosphere and spatial sophistication.

GEHRY RESIDENCE, 1978

Santa Monica, California, USA

FRANK GEHRY

The view into the kitchen atrium of Gehry's own house on a quiet street attests to how he sought to capture the quality of the existing gambrel-roofed, asbestos-shingled bungalow in an iconoclastic reconstructed shell, celebrating it as an objet trouvé. Constructed of cheap materials such as chainlink fencing, corrugated metal, and plywood, the house creates a shocking impression through the skewing of forms, caught as if in the midst of seismic activity, while acknowledging the quality of the suburban house. In receiving the Pritzker Prize in 1989, Gehry reflected on the impact of his "artist friends" Jasper Johns, Robert Rauschenberg, Claes Oldenburg, and Ed Kienholz: "In trying to find the essence of my own expression, I fantasized that I was an artist standing before a white canvas deciding what the first move should be. That was a moment of truth."

EDRIS HOUSE, 1954

Palm Springs, California, USA

E. STEWART WILLIAMS

E. Stewart Williams wanted this residence in the Coachella Valley, commissioned by his friends Marjorie and William Edris, to look "as if it grew out of the ground rather than falling out of the sky." And indeed, the stone-and-timber three-bedroom residence is barely visible from the road, hunkering into the rocky landscape. Floor-to-ceiling glass on the house's perimeters brings the outside inside. The house helped to define Desert Modernism, defying midcentury Modern's reputation for being "cold," in part due to the interior's generous wood cladding, and its main living space being focused on the fireplace, like a cave. Williams's custom-designed light fixtures—seen in, for example, an entryway planter containing projecting steel light rods which emulate natural forms—reinforce the primal feeling.

TIMBER HOUSE, 2014
Neumarkt in der Oberpfalz, Germany

KÜHNLEIN ARCHITEKTUR

These two gable-ended volumes are connected centrally, giving the building an H-shaped plan and creating two courtyards. One wing houses bedrooms, the other a completely open-plan living space. In the sleeping wing, a veil of untreated larch strips seems to entirely obscure the windows, offering privacy and giving the building a monolithic aesthetic. In the other, large openings look onto the courtyards formed between the two blocks. Larch is a popular wood for building, because it is resistant to rotting—even in contact with the ground. It is waterproof and durable, and it weathers to a handsome and uniform silver-gray. Inside, there is more timber on the walls and oak on the floors, complemented by the use of a beautiful untreated copper in all fittings—from the light switches to the faucets.

DELAWIE RESIDENCE NO. 1, 1958

San Diego, California, USA

HOMER DELAWIE

Born in 1927, Delawie was the first licensed architect who graduated from the new architectural school at Cal Poly, San Luis Obispo, in 1951. He worked with the Modernist Lloyd Ruocco starting in 1956, and set up his own practice in 1961. Delawie designed sixty private residences and several major public buildings around San Diego. This award-winning post-and-beam home, also known as the Boxcar House, was built for himself and his wife and young son when they had little money. It is only 17 feet (5.2 meters) wide on a tiny plot, perching above the harbor. He crammed four bedrooms and two bathrooms into an L-shaped volume wrapped around a gnarled old peppertree. "It's one of my favorite houses. I have three favorites," said Delawie—the others being two more residences he designed for his family.

HUNT HOUSE, 1957
Malibu, California, USA

CRAIG ELLWOOD

Elegant and minimal, this weekend house on the coast in Malibu is artfully arranged over two levels. Credited to the flamboyant and hedonistic Craig Ellwood—who came to prominence during the post-World War II expansion of Los Angeles in the 1940s—the house design is actually thought to have been by Jerrold Lomax, while Ellwood's practice designed the furnishings. At street level, two boxlike garages with driveways connect to the main house via a walkway. The H-shaped plan features bedrooms at the rear and a glass-fronted, open-plan kitchen and living area, with a terrace that overlooks the beach. Seen as a milestone in the "less is more" movement in Californian architecture, the Hunt House also marks a point when Modernism transitioned to be more about lifestyle than function.

HOUSE SH, 2005

Tokyo, Tokyo Prefecture, Japan

HIROSHI NAKAMURA & NAP

House SH is situated in a dense Tokyo streetscape, but it is devoid of residential detail. Instead, it offers an intriguingly blank facade to the street, save for its signature "bulge." A defining feature is the void to the north of the plan, which draws daylight deep into the building from a large light well in the roof. Throughout the building, space, function, and privacy are not defined in conventional terms but by the strength and character of the light. The living and dining area on the second floor is large and open plan, and focused on the curved bulge that intrigues from the street. This unusual form is embraced as both sculpture and furniture—residents are able to physically interact with the structure by lying and sitting on the walls. Nakamura has created a house with which the family can actively engage.

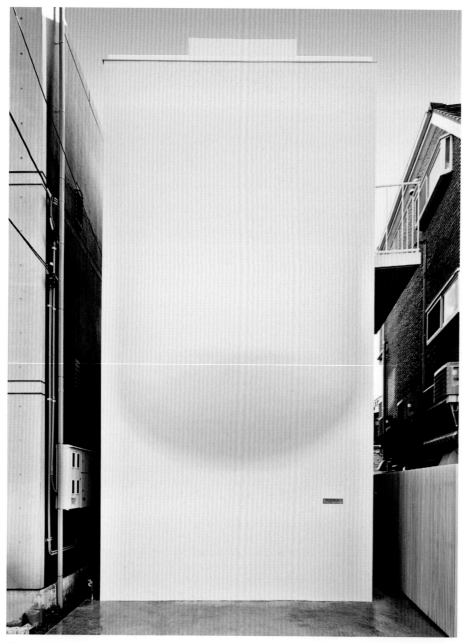

MAISON SAINT-CYR, 1903

Brussels, Belgium

GUSTAVE STRAUVEN

A long-time collaborator of Victor Horta, Gustave Strauven went on to develop his own distinctly flamboyant style of second-generation Art Nouveau. The Maison Saint-Cyr—Strauven's most exuberant design—is characterized by its extraordinary, narrow street facade. Despite the restricted width of the site, Strauven used its extreme proportions to celebrate his artistry. The sculptural relief of the surface, while providing decorative embellishment, also introduces light and external space into the building via its full-width balconies and full-height windows. All of this creates a general impression of lightness, emphasized by the dramatic, filigree "crown" at the top of the building. In this project, Strauven pushed both the materials and his artistic expression to the limit. In doing so, he undoubtedly created one of the most seductive buildings of his time.

MILAM RESIDENCE, 1961

Jacksonville, Florida, USA

PAUL RUDOLPH

This home on Ponte Vedra Beach has an indefinable otherworldly quality about it; the Modernist building seems elevated above the everyday. Independent from the structure behind it, the rectangles and squares of the orthogonal facade occasionally relate to interior rooms at various levels by the formation of a brise-soleil, making the design both visually stimulating and functional. Inside, Rudolph used various spatial manipulations, altering ceiling heights to create different moods in the home according to use. Originally, he wanted to construct the house from poured-in-place concrete, but this proved prohibitively expensive. He managed to halve the costs by using concrete blocks, which create the impression that the building is merging into the pale adjacent sand. The residence was added to the U.S. National Register of Historic Places in 2016.

VIZCAYA, 1922

Miami, Florida, USA

FRANCIS BURRALL HOFFMAN JR. & PAUL CHALFIN

Vizcaya is a palazzo built, not in the Veneto, but in Miami on the shore of Biscayne Bay. Its owner, James Deering, was an heir to a Midwestern farm equipment fortune who chose to retire to the comparatively untamed subtropical wilderness that was Miami in the early twentieth century. Interior designer, Paul Chalfin, hired Francis Burrall Hoffman to design a house. Hoffman, however, was constricted in his choice of form, given Chalfin's proposed recreations of Italian Renaissance interiors, often using original wall elements and treasures shipped over from Europe. Designed around a palazzo-style courtyard (enclosed in the 1980s with a dark pyramid roof), the house became a virtual museum of the decorative arts. There are also Italian gardens designed by Diego Suarez and, just offshore, a stone barge by Sterling Calder.

TOWER HOUSE, 1966

Tokyo, Tokyo Prefecture, Japan

TAKAMITSU AZUMA

Built on a site roughly the size of two car parking spaces, the five-level, exposed concrete Tower House is a masterpiece of the minimal urban dwelling. Designed for the architect and his family, the rooms of this house are stacked on top of each other, connected only by a winding open stair as a continuous area with no interior doors. The compact interior space is opened up visually by a large picture window between the second and third floors. The house is situated on a boulevard created in preparation for the 1964 Tokyo Olympics, and expresses Azuma's "desire to remain steadfast in the middle of the city," to embrace the chaotic city head-on, and overcome its high land prices. The house stands strong as a monument to the commitment of a very individual architect.

PRAXIS HOME, 1970
Mexico City, Mexico

AGUSTÍN HERNÁNDEZ NAVARRO

Agustín Hernández Navarro's own studio and home is suspended above a steep void and accessed from an exposed footbridge. It expresses the architect's fascination with pre-Hispanic motifs, which are a consistent theme in his work, and the concrete house recalls two interlocking pyramids which seem to defy gravity. Equally recognizable is his use of materials en masse, which creates architecture with a monumental sense of scale. The house has a "canopy" of living spaces, rooted to the site by a sturdy concrete column, and imagined by Navarro as a tree. Circular and triangular apertures incise the concrete facades, and these cutout primary geometries are a feature of Navarro's projects. A polished steel entrance leads to first-floor living, dining, and studio spaces, with bedrooms on the second floor leading to a roof deck.

HADAWAY HOUSE, 2013

Whistler, British Columbia, Canada

PATKAU ARCHITECTS

Located in the Whistler Valley, this ski chalet is positioned on a wedge-shaped site at the top of a steep slope. "It's a spaceship in the middle of log cabins," said the architects. Strict regulations for the locality meant that instead of the house being designed from the inside out, according to needs, the envelope took priority, meeting stipulations about height, recesses, and cladding. Its sharply angled roof keeps the snow off. Cardboard models were made first, translated into 3-D software, then reconfigured to accommodate interior spatial requirements. The main level of the house consists of a large living area leading to an outdoor deck with views of the valley below. A crevicelike aperture runs beneath the highest roof ridge, allowing daylight to permeate the insides of the building.

EDGELAND HOUSE, 2012
Austin, Texas, USA

BERCY CHEN STUDIO

Edgeland House is part architecture as installation, part attempt to restore a former brownfield site in Austin, Texas. Adopting the Native American pit house as a model, the architects dug seven feet (two meters) into the ground. A turf roof disguises the house as a simple green mound from the street side, ensuring privacy. But it also keeps the building warm in winter and cool in summer. Two separate volumes, one for sleeping and one for living, lack any kind of connecting hallway, to encourage the owners to spend more time outside. The Edgeland House is sited in an area that has been scarred considerably by industry, and, according to the architects, the project is "about healing the land." Following its completion in 2012, forty local species of wildflowers and other plants were reintroduced to the site.

VILLA VALS, 2009

Graubünden, Switzerland

SeARCH & CHRISTIAN MÜLLER ARCHITECTS

Set on an alpine slope in Graubünden, this innovative subterranean house has been completely embedded into a hillside to minimize its impact on the landscape. It is only accessible via a nearby barn structure which provides an additional living and sleeping area. The barn connects to a tunnel that leads to the house. From outside, the glazed facade appears as a concave ellipse, scooped out from the mountain. The form creates a sheltered courtyard area featuring a hot tub and outdoor seating. Designed by Bjarne Mastenbroek and Christian Müller of the studios SeARCH and CMA, respectively, the house has raw concrete interiors which are counterbalanced by oak paneling and doors, and natural stone steps. The Villa Vals has been furnished by Dutch designers, including Demakersvan and Hella Jongerius.

SOFT AND HAIRY HOUSE, 1994

Tsukuba, Ibaraki, Japan

USHIDA FINDLAY

A one-story, concrete spiral tube surrounds a courtyard which is linked to a roof garden covered with plants amid projecting skylights. The linear interior space within the tube is articulated ambiguously so that it maintains an organic continuity. However, the interior is also uniquely designed to establish a series of theatrical spaces, such as a blue, egg-shaped bathroom, a cozy study surrounded with bookshelves and spiral drapes, and a bedroom softly lit by a skylight above the bed. The architects, quoting Salvador Dalí's words literally, intended to make a "soft and hairy house" where a personal illusion could be explored and realized within various dreamlike settings. The house reflects the expression of diversity in its inhabitants' lifestyle. Its highly subjective character precludes any objective criticism.

HOUSE IN LEIRIA, 2010

Leiria, Portugal

AIRES MATEUS

This house overlooks the city of Leiria in Portugal's Centro region, and its blank white-rendered facades are a typical attribute of Aires Mateus's work. In the form of an archetypal gabled house, it has no doors or windows apart from an entrance at the east end. The home is mostly built underground. The kitchen, living room, and dining room are on the ground floor, while bedrooms are in the basement, illuminated and ventilated by three light wells that are cut out of the ground and visible in the garden. A void excised from the center of the house is not only a striking visual element, but also brings in more light and allows for a patio on the basement level and roof deck on the top floor. The house has a cool minimalism, which hides a complex interior that is open to light and air.

FIELD HOUSE, 2006

Ellington, Wisconsin, USA

WENDELL BURNETTE ARCHITECTS

The Field House sits amid the agricultural landscape in Outagamie County, Wisconsin. Its form is composed of a zinc-galvanized orthogonal box inspired by vernacular farm buildings and silos. The ridge pattern of the interlocking cladding recalls the regular rows of nearby planted crops. South- and east-facing elevations are extensively glazed to maximize the warmth from the sun. For economy, all of the materials used were utilized in their existing standard dimensions, and commercial construction techniques were employed, rather than traditional residential methods. The client, an amateur astronomer, enjoys a rooftop observatory. While this house might appear plain and utilitarian, it is the moments of wonder and connection with the landscape that make it something special to live in.

LOS TERRENOS, 2017

Monterrey, Mexico

TATIANA BILBAO

"Los Terrenos," which means "The Terrains" in Spanish, is a project by Bilbao consisting of two small buildings (with a third to be built in the future), contained within a square plot. Each of the structures serves a particular function, and is distinctive for its use of a single material, to arresting visual effect—such as mirrored glass, rammed earth, and clay bricks (and wood for the third building). The building pictured here, which contains the living, kitchen, and dining space, is sheathed in mirrored glass. Multiple reflections of the trees and sky dissolve a clear sense of outline, boundary, and space; the gabled roof, for example, is barely perceptible. To prevent overheating, the interior is partly lined with plywood. The sleeping area is in a separate building, constructed of clay bricks and rammed earth.

MORIYAMA HOUSE, 2005

Tokyo, Tokyo Prefecture, Japan

RYUE NISHIZAWA

Yasuo Moriyama is a sort of urban hermit with an encyclopedic knowledge of culture and the arts. His house, designed by one of the founding partners of Japanese architecture studio SANAA, Pritzer Prize-winner Ryue Nishizawa, fragments the idea of "a house" into ten separate blocks, creating a sort of microcity. Moriyama lives in four of these, and the others are rented out. Varying from one to three stories high, the volumes are sparsely furnished, filled instead with books, DVDs, and art. One box contains simply a sink and bathtub. The Moriyama House represents a radical decomposition of the conventional home, and is considered to be one of the most important houses of the twenty-first century. A 2017 film, called *Moriyama-san*, by Louise Lemoine and Ila Bêka, documented one week in the life of Moriyama at his home.

BAKKAFLÖT 1, 1968

Garðabær, Iceland

HÖGNA SIGURÐARDÓTTIR

Högna Sigurðardóttir practised in France but designed several domestic houses in Iceland. Located in a suburban street in a settlement south of Reykjavík, Bakkaflöt 1 seems mostly submerged in green turf, with only its roof visible: three manmade mounds almost conceal the front facade. These reference traditional turf-roofed Icelandic houses, updated in a Modernist idiom; the ground literally rises up to hug the house. The low, simple house is made of exposed concrete, cast in situ. Inside, the open-plan layout is based around a huge central fireplace, and a skylight generously illuminates the space. Much of the furniture—the sofa, the beds, and even the bathtub—is cast from concrete, creating a connection between inside and outside. The overall sense is one of being burrowed in and protected from the harsh Icelandic elements.

BRIDGE HOUSE, 2011

Rotterdam, The Netherlands

123DV

The rural region of Achterhoek, in the eastern Netherlands, is characterized by gently rolling hills, open farmland, and tree-lined avenues. This two-story luxury villa, designed by 123dv, takes the form of a simple, elongated rectangle with a minimalist glazed facade, situated in the middle of open parkland. The lower floor is almost totally sunk into two manmade mounds made from earth taken from the estate to make the ground less fertile. Being nestled into the earth gives the Bridge House a sense of protection and snug integration with the landscape. Front and rear entrances are located in a chasm between the two hills. Along with solar panels, the villa has its own well and reuses rainwater; thermal energy is stored to heat the ceilings and floors, and Heat Mirror glass cools down the interiors.

TILL HOUSE, 2014

Navidad, Chile

WMR ARQUITECTOS

Cut into a deep shelf on a Los Arcos promontory, a typical Chilean coastal landscape, this small-scale weekend shelter is designed to engage with the outdoors. The roar of the sea, surrounding the retreat on three sides, is constant. With this in mind, one-third of the house's depth is given over to a lattice-shaded open terrace for lounging and sea gazing, while the rest is for sleeping and eating. In addition, the entire roof is a massive open deck reached by a walkway which extends from the cliffside. The Till House is invisible from the road. Maximal glazing provides panoramic views, natural lighting, and sea breezes, while some privacy is afforded to the rear quarters of the house with screening panels. The interior is arranged largely to be open-plan, with individual rooms sectioned off with shelving units.

CLIFF HOUSE, 2010

Nova Scotia, Canada

MACKAY-LYONS
SWEETAPPLE ARCHITECTS

"Pure, dignified, poetic and beautiful" is how Brian Mackay-Lyons's work was described by the jury of the Royal Architectural Institute of Canada when he won a Gold Medal in 2015. The Cliff House exemplifies these qualities. The first of several projects to be built on a 455-acre (184-hectare) property on the Atlantic coast in Nova Scotia, it is a modest interpretation of the archetypal "cabin in the landscape" form. Low-budget, using vernacular building techniques—a wood-frame structure with a cedar lap exterior—it is intended to be a didactic project on the lived experience of inhabiting a landscape. The house contains a double-height living and dining room, and a mezzanine bedroom. Viewed from the rear it appears as a snug box, but rather the structure is thrust out over a cliff, supported by steel I-beams.

HOUSE MOBY-DICK, 2003

Espoo, Finland

ARKKITEHDIT NRT OY

This house, designed by Arkkitehdit NRT Oy co-founder Jyrki Tasa, hugs an outcrop of rocks on a small hill in Espoo, northwest of Helsinki. It is situated in a low-density housing area, but its choice of plot and its whalelike, biomorphic form make it the antithesis of ordinary suburban design. Actually, it is V-shaped in plan: the sweeping curve that suggests Herman Melville's cetacean is on the east-facing elevation, seen on the approach to the house's entrance, which is reached by a metal footbridge spanning the rocks. Constructed with a steel frame, both terminations of the "V" are glazed areas that flood the house with light. The more public-facing areas are covered with a white-painted plywood skin, which has been molded to twist and flex. Interior walls are rectangular in section, forming a dynamic contrast with the outer shell.

SCHMINKE HOUSE, 1933

Löbau, Germany

HANS SCHAROUN

The canted relationship between the north–south orientation of the central block of this house and its two side wings, which follow the site boundaries at an angle, gives an inherent dynamism to this design. Scharoun exploits this characteristic with transparent walls and double-height spaces. His architecture depended on interpretation of site (note here the cantilever off the garden wall), and of the functions that a building would accommodate, in opposition to preconceived Corbusian forms. The imminent Nazi regime—during which Scharoun remained in Germany—repressed the consummation of the refined relationship between form and function he achieved here. After World War II, Scharoun became Director of the Building and Housing Department for Greater Berlin, setting the stage for his greatest works and public buildings.

ST JOSEPH HOUSE, 2007

St Andrä-Wördern, Austria

WOLFGANG TSCHAPELLER
ARCHITEKTEN

This house is sited on the edge of St Andrä-Wördern, a small town by the River Danube. The project form and materials distinguish it from the town's saddle-roofed houses, and the building is elevated on stilts in case of floods. Generous windows are inserted into the concrete shell, and irregularly shaped glass panes are set flush into the walls. Steel stairs, more akin to a ladder, lead up to the entrance on the south side. A second white form, independent from the outer shell, is set within the concrete box. Within the rectangular volume, there is a diagonal flow from the entrance toward the northwest and along the kitchen. The internal staircase follows this movement in the opposite direction. Upstairs, two rooms are situated on either side of the diagonal. Over this is a small lookout space with a slightly tilted silhouette.

BURST*003, 2005

North Haven, New South Wales, Australia

SYSTEMARCHITECTS

Douglas Gauthier with Jeremy Edmiston, as SYSTEMarchitects, designed this prefabricated holiday home on the eastern coast of Australia to be full of small details that celebrate its purpose as a place to surf, relax, and have fun. Perched on stilts, it has a plywood rib structure. The wood sheets were delivered to the site with the components numbered, scored, and holes cut, ready for assembly. The supporting ribs beneath the house feature voids for storing surfboards and wetsuits. The house has two key elements: a living room, which focuses inward and has an off-center peak in the roof; and a rear dining room area, which allows light to enter from two directions into the space. This results in a complicated volume with ever-changing sections. The exterior is decorated with cartoonish floral reliefs inspired by the pattern on a bikini.

HUGO AND BRIGITTE EPPICH HOUSE, 1979

West Vancouver, British Columbia, Canada

ARTHUR ERICKSON

Erickson designed this home in the desirable Vancouver suburb of British Properties for a steel manufacturer and his family. Taking a decade to complete, the project aimed to push steel to its creative limits, with everything, including furniture and fittings, made in Hugo Eppich's plant. The home's three levels cascade over a slope, and each floor's curved, glazed terminations give the building a cloudlike appearance. A stream flanks the house, while boundaries between inside and out merge: glass facades with white-painted steel structural beams frame gorgeous views of trees, water, and sky; and the home steps down into a verdant, tree-filled valley where bears have been known to visit. The effect is dreamlike but always practical: Brigitte Eppich once remarked that she wanted to "see the children playing even when I was ironing."

THE HOUSE ON THE CLIFF, 2015

Granada, Spain

GILBARTOLOME ARCHITECTS

Embedded within a cliff face, this Gaudíesque home ripples over the contours of a vertiginous forty-two-degree slope. It uses the natural cooling of the earth to maintain a constant temperature of 67 degrees Fahrenheit (19.5 degrees Celsius) throughout the year. The lower level is the living area, with pool and cantilevering terrace, which has views across the Mediterranean sea; the upper has three bedrooms with views framed by the sensuous roof. The house is covered with an undulating double shell of reinforced concrete that sits upon a moldable metal frame. Commissioned during a recession, in an area with a high unemployment rate, the project employed local artisans when possible. The rolling roof framework is handcrafted, as are the zinc tiles on top, which give it the appearance of a dragon's scaly skin.

ATHAN HOUSE, 1988

Monbulk, Victoria , Australia

EDMOND & CORRIGAN

With its razor-sharp lines and theatrical, pinstriped cladding, the Athan House makes a remarkable contrast to its surrounding eucalypt forest. "The building in some ways represents an urban idea relocated to the Australian bush," say its architects, Edmond & Corrigan, a practice that bucks the "outback" trend of much contemporary Australian architecture in favour of a more urbane approach. The residence was built as an unofficial hotel of sorts in which the clients' extended family of teenage and grown-up children could live together, yet privately. Designed like a medieval city or walled fortress, complete with its own entry bridge, the house is a labyrinth of strangely angled rooms, twisting staircases, and knife-edged balconies—a real maze of spaces that offered family members the option of being alone or congregating.

SUMMER HOUSE, 1953

Muuratsalo, Finland

ALVAR AALTO

In a forest overlooking a lake in north-central Finland, this summer house was both a retreat and a test bed where one of the most important architects of the twentieth century developed his own particular contribution to Modernism. Under the influence of this sylvan, Scandinavian setting, the house marks a decisive shift away from the more familiar Modernist planar surfaces toward consciously varied tactile and aesthetic effects, a principal feature of the Finnish tradition in which Alvar Aalto was pre-eminent. The composition of the house is simple: two equal wings at right angles enclose the courtyard, with a separate guest annex. Fifty different types of brick and ceramic tile line the courtyard. Sensibility to site and manipulation of surface are hallmarks that extend to Aalto's large public commissions.

DEANERY GARDENS, 1902

Sonning, England, UK

SIR EDWIN LUTYENS

A large, long roof presides over the vertical features of this house, which combines formal principles with a response to function. The two-story bay window declares the importance of the hall within, while presenting an axial relationship with the commanding roof. Lutyens was the pre-eminent British architect of the early twentieth century. His fascination with axial compositions would eventually steer him toward Classicism, but at Deanery Gardens essentially vernacular elements are arranged on axes to create one of the most sophisticated houses in the Arts and Crafts tradition. Hidden from the public by an ancient wall, the house is orientated toward this, its most private side. The Edwardian taste was for public ostentation, but this house exudes an enduring image of domesticity that suited the client, *Country Life* magazine founder, Edward Hudson.

VILLA GADELIUS, 1961

Lidingö, Sweden

RALPH ERSKINE

Ralph Erskine was a British architect who did much of his work in Sweden; he is best known in Britain for his low-cost housing, such as Byker Wall estate (1982) in Newcastle and the Ark office building (1992) in Hammersmith. Villa Gadelius is a split-level three-story house for developer Taro Gadelius, situated on the island of Lidingö, in the inner archipelago of Stockholm. Hillside rock wraps around part of the dwelling, and it has a turf roof. Erskine designed the garage and storage areas of the house as a buffer zone against the chill north winds, and the house is funnel-shaped to cope with the harsh elements: the south part of the house is extended in the east-west direction and living spaces are double-height so they have access to the low winter sun. Concrete beams frame key entrances and act as pergolas, and there are two funnel-like chimneys.

GELON HANNA HOUSE, 2013
Kent, England, UK

SIMON CONDER ASSOCIATES

A windy, bleak expanse of shingle, the hamlet of Dungeness is the most desertlike environment in the UK. Situated on the south coast between East Sussex and Kent, it is home to a nuclear power station and has a distinctive end-of-the-world feel. Conder was commissioned to upgrade this 1930s fisherman's hut as part of the unique settlement's "bodged [botched] squatter architecture," as he put it. Tight planning laws stipulate that new houses can only be built on the footprint of existing structures and cannot exceed them proportionally. Therefore, the hut was stripped and rebuilt, and covered in an insulating black rubber coating—the first use of it in the UK—rather than the layers of felt and tar used on nearby houses. The home's best views are from the cantilevering bathroom, from a bathtub vantage point.

BLACK DESERT HOUSE, 2014

Yucca Valley, California, USA

OLLER & PEJIC ARCHITECTURE

Built on an isolated site, in a niche carved between rock formations in the California High Desert, this project was driven by the client's goal to build a house like a shadow. Observing that in the desert a shadow is often the only resting place for the eye, the intention of a black house was to act as a similar respite, not only from the desert sun, but from the stress of urban life. In order to mitigate the heat absorbed by the black concrete exterior, deeper and wider insulation cavities were combined with sprayed foam insulation. Spread out over a single level, rooms are arranged along a linear program. The living room, defined around the client's mandate that it was to be a "chic sleeping bag," affords panoramic views of the landscape. Interiors are also executed in black and gray so that the inside of the house, too, recedes into the shadows.

MOUNTAIN TREE HOUSE, 2001

Dillard, Georgia, USA

MACK SCOGIN MERRILL
ELAM ARCHITECTS

Designed to be a weekend retreat, this wood-and-steel-framed home is one of three structures in the Mountain House Modern complex designed by Mack Scogin Merrill Elam. Set amid a poplar wood in the foothills of the Southern Appalachian Mountains, the Mountain Tree House consists of simple interlocking volumes. A concrete garage is built into the hillside with an adjacent work yard; a steel box with a bedroom and bathroom cantilevers above it, with translucent glass walls; the bedroom leads out onto a long, narrow, elevated slate-and-Corten-steel deck, which takes a right-angled turn into the forest. Beneath this, there is a bamboo garden, with the tall trees here penetrating the deck. The architects describe the Mountain Tree House as "an inside-outside thing, but also an up-down and heavy-light thing."

FALL HOUSE, 2013

Big Sur, California, USA

FOUGERON ARCHITECTURE

Perched almost 262 feet (80 meters) above the Pacific Ocean on a verdant cliff face, this long, thin house has two main facades: the south is clad in copper, while the north is glass. The house is composed of two volumes joined together by a glazed atrium that serves as a library and den, with the smaller of the two volumes cantilevered toward the ocean. An open-plan interior sets the tone of the house, which is at once transparent and secluded. Level changes within demarcate the different living spaces. Terraces and patios occupy the boundary of the property, which is also home to a delicate ecosystem. As part of the sustainable approach to this house, local and drought-resistant vegetation has been planted to reduce soil erosion and encourage wildlife to resettle on the building's isolated site.

HÄUSLER HOUSE, 1995

Hard, Austria

BAUMSCHLAGER EBERLE
ARCHITEKTEN

The tough concrete and crisp geometry of the Häusler House, by Baumschlager Eberle, turns its back on the red-tiled, pitched-roof suburban architecture of its neighbors. Essentially introverted, the house is entered through a large opening in the solid concrete frontage, which is actually a passageway that splits the building in two and can be closed off with a sliding wooden gate to create a courtyard. A further internal courtyard is set within the larger half of the house, but here, in contrast to the exterior, the detailing is more delicate and finely scaled. The fortress-like appearance is re-emphasized at the rear, where a protective concrete grid is set beyond the glazed elevation of the louvered-timber house itself. A series of open-air terraces at varying levels is strictly contained within this gridded zone.

CASA KLOTZ, 1991

Tongoy, Chile

MATHIAS KLOTZ

This weekend retreat by Mathias Klotz is an exercise in abstraction, pure geometry, and clean proportion. The house—a double-cube volume—sits along the empty beach at Tongoy, a seaside town north of Santiago. The wall that faces onto the access road is left intentionally blank; in contrast, the rear elevation has full-height windows overlooking the bay. The first floor has two galleries: one containing stairs, a bathroom, and a small bedroom; the other the main bedroom and double-height living and dining areas. Upstairs are additional guest rooms and terraces, all of which face the ocean panorama. To emphasize its object-like quality, Klotz raised the house 1 foot (30 centimeters) off the ground on short stilts. Rough pine planks on the wooden structure's exterior give it the air of a rustic summer camp, more than a polished vacation home.

HOUSE ON THE CLIFF, 2012

Alicante, Spain

FRAN SILVESTRE ARQUITECTOS

The smooth and cubic forms of the House on the Cliff are rather astonishing against the dark, irregular mass of the rocks it clings to. Designed by Fran Silvestre Arquitectos as a single concrete structure, its stunning horizontality is a perfect contrast to the mountain's vertical flanks. Walls are covered with stucco to create the white facade. A projecting 60-foot-long (18-meter-long) balcony creates an enormous viewing platform: this is a place to gaze out over the Mediterranean Sea and amble back and forth, but not exert oneself. Its form and location mean that it is not designed for frenetic, everyday activity; in fact, it is calculated precisely to slow its inhabitants down, persuading them into an exquisite torpor. The architects envisioned the House on the Cliff as the ideal place to do nothing.

VILLA E-1027, 1929

Roquebrune, France

EILEEN GRAY & JEAN BADOVICI

This house, which Gray built for herself, is evidence of her allegiance to the cubist forms of Parisian builders, adapted to a Mediterranean climate: it is a simple regular volume, subdivided according to functional demands, in which the interior and furniture are realized in modern materials (celluloid, fiber-cement, aluminum). Its name corresponds to the coded initials of its creators (E=Eileen, 10=J, 2=B and 7=G). As a member of the Union des Artistes Modernes, Gray associated with progressivist designers such as Robert Mallet-Stevens and Jean Prouvé. Gray built very little, yet this house is a refined example of the International Style. As she wrote in a 1929 issue of *L'Architecture vivante*: "The house to be described should not be considered a perfect house, when all problems are resolved. It is only an attempt, a moment in a more general research."

FALLINGWATER, 1939

Bear Run, Pennsylvania, USA

FRANK LLOYD WRIGHT

With its dramatic, horizontal concrete slabs cantilevered over the roaring crescendo of a waterfall, Fallingwater symbolizes both the romance of nature and the triumph of man. At first glance, the horizontal emphasis is reminiscent of the prevalent International Modernism of the time; however, the natural materials and hand-crafted details—evident in the stacked stone walls—betray its roots in the Arts and Crafts tradition, while the plan is borrowed from Wright's earlier Prairie House-type, with volumes developing from a central core. Inside, the contrast between man and nature continues: the polished flagstone floor appears as though a river had flowed over it for centuries, yet the recessed ceilings float overhead as manmade works of art. Fallingwater is arguably the most important twentieth-century house in the USA.

CASA PITE, 2005

Papudo, Chile

SMILJAN RADIC

Located two hours north of Santiago, the Casa Pite was built as a family weekend retreat. The house is actually a complex of different zones: a central living area with master bedroom, a guest cottage, a swimming pool, and a glazed pavilion, which houses the children's bedrooms—perched on the edge of a cliff. This simple, elongated, one-story volume is the closest of the structures to the sea. Each one of these sectors—symmetrically composed in themselves—are connected by platforms and exterior ramps. The clients wanted the dwelling to be invisible from the road, so the architect's partner, sculptor Marcela Correa, placed eleven basalt rocks on a platform above. Over time, the property will further blend with the landscape, as yellow grasslands invade the stonework of the pavements and wide terraces.

VILLA LA SARACENA, 1957

Santa Marinella, Italy

LUIGI MORETTI

In the coastal town of Santa Marinella, Luigi Moretti designed this introverted villa for the socialite princess Luciana Pignatelli. It was completed three years after her marriage to Prince Don Nicolò Maria Pignatelli Aragon Cortès. A gate from the street leads into a circular walled garden. Across from this are two heavy abstract forms—an elliptical tower on the left, enclosing the sleeping areas, and on the right, a wing topped with a cantilevering, partly curved roof terrace. Entering this side, a corridor leads to the dining and living spaces overlooking the sea. The beach can be accessed via a private grotto, which has an exquisite Modernist gate designed by sculptor Claire Falkenstein in tangled ironwork. Moretti wrote, in 1970, of the house: "This is a jealous house, 'Saracen,' in its affections and thoughts … it is a house that calms the restless."

WICHITA HOUSE, 1946
Wichita, Kansas, USA

RICHARD BUCKMINSTER FULLER

This circular, aluminum, single-unit dwelling was a prototype for a mass-producible, lightweight house with pre-installed services, capable of being transported and erected anywhere. It built on Fuller's visionary ideas first explored in his 1927 Dymaxion House project, which was technologically ahead of its time. The floors were to be laid on pneumatic bladders, suspended by tensile cables from a central mast anchored in a base that contained septic and fuel tanks. The external walls were to be of transparent plastic with curtains of aluminum sheeting, and the doors operated by photo-electric cells. It was Fuller's commitment to industrialization of the building process as the key to "solving total humanity's evolutionary shelter problems," while respecting the earth's resources, that underpinned his designs.

THE QUEST, 2016

Swanage, England, UK

STRÖM ARCHITECTS

At the heart of this house, which replaced a bungalow, are quality and simplicity. Located in the country park of Durlston, Purbeck, the new house for a retired couple was rotated to provide better views. A single story accommodated the couple's needs and those of their disabled daughter. The site, a former quarry, featured dramatic differences in levels, and the design cleverly negotiates these: a driveway with a retaining wall made of Purbeck stone grounds the composition; to the left of this is a sunken parking area. The residence cantilevers over the retaining wall; two enormous planes—floor and roof—are infilled with timber, leaving the concrete frame visible. A chimney bisects the house and adds pleasing verticality. The home is unpretentious, beautifully made, and in tune with its surroundings.

PLUS, 2009

Izu, Shizuoka, Japan

MOUNT FUJI ARCHITECTS

Nestled into the side of Izu-San mountain, this simple dwelling, to be used as a weekend house, sits sensitively in its environment. It is formed of two long cuboid volumes arranged in a cross, and appears as if gently pinned to the terrain. The plot was of limited size and on a small ridge. It therefore made sense to have one of the volumes cantilevering outward and the other sitting astride it. The lower structure houses the bedrooms, and living space is in the upper story. Clad in white marble, the Plus house's pure linear forms seem to emerge naturally from the mountainside, which is covered in Japanese oak and cherry trees. "It's an abstraction of nature," said architect Masahiro Harada. Living areas on the upper floor, and the terrace jutting out perpendicularly below, take in endless views of the Pacific Ocean.

STEINHAUS, BEGUN IN 1986

Carinthia, Austria

GÜNTHER DOMENIG

The Steinhaus is part house, part architecture school, part ongoing architectural expression. Working with the metaphorical expressive shapes used by Deconstructivists, it represents an ambiguous "bird," and yet is built of materials so rough they can draw blood. The house, which is described extensively in a series of scribbled drawings, was developed as a manmade mound split into cliffs and a ravine, with expressive steel and concrete outcrops. The entrance is via a deep path, leading to a glass cylinder. The building is arranged around a spiralling plan where the formal organization of the rooms has been deliberately disrupted. Along the route is sleeping accommodation, or "baskets," a wedge-shaped eating area, and a path leading out to the sky and terminating in a take-off ramp for the apocryphal bird, aimed across the lake.

DRAGSPEL HOUSE, 2004

Smolmark, Sweden

NATRUFIED ARCHITECTURE

"Dragspel," which means "Accordion" in Swedish, references the concertinalike folds of red cedarwood of this summerhouse. But the design also resembles some fantastical horned creature that has come to rest by the side of Lake Övre Gla. An extension to a late nineteenth-century cabin, it is designed to have a minimal visual impact in this nature reserve, and windows are hidden within the skin of the structure. In the summer, the front part of the cabin can extend outward to cantilever over a stream, retracting into a cocoon shape in the winter. The interior walls are lined with pine lattice and reindeer pelts, to create a typically Nordic atmosphere. Boris Zeisser's practice, called Natrufied—an amalgamation of the words nature and petrified— frequently uses biomimicry in its designs to intriguing effect.

LAWSON-WESTEN HOUSE, 1993

Brentford, California, USA

ERIC OWEN MOSS

The spiraling staircase at the heart of the Lawson-Westen House offers a dramatic moment of architectural abstraction. It is symbolic of the intricacy and disjunction not just of this house, but of much contemporary Californian architecture. The clients for this house said they wanted "room to breathe," and they had a preference for high-ceilinged living rooms. The house form is generated by the circular kitchen, which is literally the central hearth where cooking and entertaining take place. Above this, the open staircase has balconies looking back down on to the kitchen and double-height living space, as well as views out through the irregular, strangely shaped windows. With the Lawson-Westen House, Eric Owen Moss created a house of enormous spatial complexity and unexpected architectural anomalies.

GROSSE GLÜCKERT HAUS, 1901
Darmstadt, Germany

JOSEF OLBRICH

A characterful building set in the leafy suburbs of Darmstadt, the Glückert Haus is the best preserved of the many houses Olbrich built after he was invited to join an artists' colony there. Like all his buildings in Darmstadt, the house is a total work of art: the exterior was highly decorated (you can just see the stylized trees on the gable end, but the mural above the porch was never completed); the interior, heavily embellished. Julius Glückert, who commissioned the house, used it as a furniture showroom, and Olbrich went on to build him a second home to live in. Darmstadt was at the heart of the Secessionist movement of which Olbrich was a chief exponent. The movement is named after the Secession exhibition building in Vienna, designed by Olbrich in 1898 as a radical alternative to the more traditional Academy of Fine Arts.

THE GLASS PAVILION, 2015

Granada, Spain

OFIS ARHITEKTI

In an area of Spain where local architecture responds to the harsh conditions with a traditional vernacular of troglodytic homes dug into the earth, this house stands out. The Glass Pavilion is situated in Granada's Gorafe desert, which can reach temperatures of up to 104 degrees Fahrenheit (40 degrees Celsius). It is a bold move to erect a glass pavilion in a desert of such magnitude, but it is also a testament to the progress of modernity. Guardian Glass, a special glazing coated with a near-invisible film, filters the sun's radiation almost completely, thus allowing the material to be used as structural walls; here it is used extensively on the Y-shaped floor plan. A terrace is shaded by the overhanging roof, part of which is clad in mirrored panels which reflect the landscape. This may be the sole fully panoramic desert structure to feature an indoor jacuzzi.

DESERT HOUSE, 2009

Palm Springs, California, USA

JIM JENNINGS ARCHITECTURE

This is the architect Jim Jennings and writer Therese Bissell's own desert retreat. Subverting Desert Modernism's tradition of the post-and-beam glass box which opens to the outdoors, Jennings' house is defined by an 8-foot (2.4-meter) perimeter concrete wall, which supports a steel roof structure and encases two courtyards. Everything within the wall functions as living space: the entrance courtyard—an outdoor dining area—leads to a enclosed area with sliding glass doors, which comprises the bedroom, sitting room, and kitchen. A second courtyard accommodates a lap pool. From the interior, views of the surroundings—palm trees, mountain, and sky—are framed by the floating roof and supporting wall, cropped into abstraction. What matters here is the overwhelmingly sensory experience of being contained within such spare, elegant geometry.

DOUGLAS HOUSE, 1973

Harbor Springs, Michigan, USA

RICHARD MEIER

Douglas House is situated, almost precipitously, high above Lake Michigan on a steeply sloping site. Meier designed this house early in his career, at a time when his ideas of form and color—or the absence of color, Meier's trademark—were drawn largely from his study of the purist work of Le Corbusier. Here, against the background of blue of the lake and sky and the green of the trees, Meier sought a "dramatic dialog" that would offer a contrast between the natural and the manmade, enhanced by the vivid whiteness of the house. Entered at roof level via a walkway, the house is arranged so that the lakeside view opens up as one descends to the living and dining areas, with the private spaces at the rear. This division of public and private can be discerned by the size of the windows: large for public, small for private.

PIKA HOUSE, 2006

Dunton Hot Springs, Colorado, USA

SELLDORF ARCHITECTS

This woodland tower is near Dunton Hot Springs, a rural vacation retreat. At five stories, it takes advantage of mountain views and minimizes damage to the spruce forest with a very small footprint based on the average floor area of a mountain shack. Its verticality also responds to the surrounding pine trees; a penthouse study surrounded by a roof deck crowns the house, just shy of the treeline. South and west elevations are clad in Spanish cedar and recycled Douglas fir, in arrangements reminiscent of local logging cabins. The other elevations have glazing more typical of Annabelle Selldorf's own rigorous brand of Modernism—the north facade of the tower references Mies van der Rohe's Seagram Building. Dark aluminum shutters provide shading in warmer weather, and in the winter, the house can be completely closed up.

THE MONUMENT, 1990

Joshua Tree National Park, California, USA

JOSHUA SCHWEITZER

Three asymmetrical, brightly colored cubes stand, like an oasis, on the edge of the Joshua Tree National Park. Built as a weekend retreat for the architect, the small, Neo-Primitive compound is made up of an olive-green living area, a blue bedroom suite, and an orange outdoor pavilion. The blocks are set in the landscape like manmade boulders, cut with openings at uneven angles to make the scale and composition both abstract and mysterious. While they appear to be freestanding volumes from the outside, the rooms are interconnected and flow freely. The oddly angled windows frame fragments of the extraordinary landscape. Even though the colors have been inspired by the intense hues of the local vegetation of lichen and cactus flowers, the house still contrasts dramatically with its natural setting.

DESERT NOMAD HOUSE, 2006

Tucson, Arizona, USA

RICK JOY ARCHITECTS

Tucson is home to the Saguaro National Park, best known for its spectacular saguaro cacti, which can grow up to 40 feet (12 meters) tall. The rusted steel cubes cluster in a sheltered bowl at the foot of the Tucson Mountains. Each entity consciously frames a different view through generous glazing: the bedroom affords a view of the sun rising, the living space captures the sun as it sets, and the studio concentrates on the immediate vista by framing the vegetation like a landscape painting. Slightly elevated on stilts, the three cubes emerge as friendly visitors on the land, providing shaded space for small animals. The geometry of the cube—an enduring topic of fascination for artists in the 1960s and '70s—and the naturally rusted steel-plate cladding lend the dwellings the appearance of Minimalist sculpture.

HOUSE IN THE AIR, 1991

Mexico City, Mexico

AGUSTÍN HERNÁNDEZ NAVARRO

An unconventional neighbor of the tile-and-terracotta homes in Bosques de las Lomas, this house hovers high over its steep slope, supported by two enormous concrete slabs cut through with large circles. Navarro believed that architecture should exploit the natural properties of materials and here created a taut contrast between steel in tension and exposed concrete in compression. The house is composed as an extruded steel-framed cantilever, rotated forty-five degrees and split into equal triangular quarters along its length. The principal double-height interior spaces are arranged over two levels and set below what appears to be a conventional gabled roof from within. A rooflight at the apex gives top-lit spaces; in the living rooms the light is complemented by circular windows. These bold geometric details are themes for which Navarro is known.

WIND HOUSE, 2015

Jeju-si, Jeju Province, South Korea

MOON HOON

Moon Hoon designs unusual and innovative buildings. Perhaps referencing Jeju-si's blustery climate, the tower sitting atop this grouping of stone dwellings has been compared to a giant hair dryer. (Others, however, liken it to a duck's head.) The plot here is composed of three houses designed as weekend retreats. Each has structural walls of board-formed concrete, and is enclosed by walls made of locally sourced stone. Two hunker low to the ground like the traditional houses in the region, while the third—with the tower—is two stories. Golden metallic tiles clad the tower, giving it a fantastical, slightly reptilian quality. Moon has said the form was inspired by earlier abortive designs for a wind museum. Painted in bold red, the interior has a womblike quality. "In my practice I try to have fun doing architecture," he has said.

LUMINOUS HOUSE, 2011

Nakatado, Kagawa, Japan

SHINICHI OGAWA & ASSOCIATES

Shinichi Ogawa, who won a traveling scholarship to work in the United States before returning to Japan to set up his own practice in 1986, specializes in sleek, elongated, minimalist houses. This one-story home in the Nakatado district is an orthogonal structure entered from its eastern end, where there is also a guest bedroom. Two more bedrooms are located at the opposite end. On the south side, a long courtyard runs the length of the house, and connects the living and sleeping spaces. The steel structure is clad with an opalescent glass that allows daylight to enter the home. By night, it glows softly, a strange beacon in the rural landscape. Both interior and outdoor spaces are white, and as a result, inside and outside appear to merge. For example, a porcelain floor tile utilized for the dining room is the same as that used in the courtyard.

SALZMAN HOUSE, 1952
Los Angeles, California, USA

CRAIG ELLWOOD

The Case Study House Program encouraged architects to envision new types of housing for postwar living. This project, Case Study House No. 16, is a steel-frame building notable from the street for its translucent glass panels, which also face an interior courtyard, which fronts the bedrooms. L-shaped in plan, the house is topped with a roof slab that floats over the vertical wall planes. The house features built-in furniture and a huge natural rock fireplace, which extends through glass walls to the covered patio. The project was innovative in its use of exposed steel structural framing, and floor-to-ceiling glazing took advantage of spectacular views. Of three, this is the only surviving, intact example of Ellwood's designs for the program; his built designs for No. 17 and No. 18 have both been altered through subsequent remodeling.

THE STALLER HOUSE, 1955

Los Angeles, California, USA

RICHARD NEUTRA

Designed for elegant outdoor living, 901 Bel Air Road is sited in a gated lot in leafy Bel Air, an affluent residential community. The residence is built into a hillside and is much larger than many of Neutra's other domestic commissions. The three-bedroom, six-bathroom post-and-beam house conjures a sense of lightness: a cantilevering canopy over the balcony is supported by slim pilotis, and ample outdoor terraces suggest easy living. Clerestory windows are by vertical mullions and allow for illumination into the "hill" side of the house, while glazing on the pool side reflects palm trees, blue skies, and sunsets. It is also referred to as the Levinsohn House, as movie producer Gary Levinsohn once lived there. The house was restored by Lorcan O'Herlihy Architects in 2001.

ALUMINAIRE HOUSE, 1931

Palm Springs, California, USA

A. LAWRENCE KOCHER
& ALBERT FREY

This pioneering home, also known as the "House of the Future," was designed for an exhibition organized by the Allied Arts and Industries and Architectural League of New York in 1931. It was the first steel and aluminum house built in the United States, and one of the earliest examples of the budding International Style. It was an affordable, lightweight *maision minimum*, which could be mass-produced to solve city housing shortages. Swiss-born architect Frey had trained under Le Corbusier, and Kocher was managing editor of *Architectural Record* magazine at the time. The Corbusian influence is clear in its prefabrication, and the metallic exterior recalls Buckminster Fuller's designs. Having seen several owners in different locations and fallen into disrepair, in 2017 it found a forever home at Downtown Park in Palm Springs.

LANDA RESIDENCE, 1997

Manhattan Beach, California, USA

MORPHOSIS

The Landa Residence demonstrates Morphosis' preoccupations with the particularity of materials and detail-oriented construction. A meditation on volume as the primary means of both establishing and transgressing boundaries developed out of the existing site restrictions of a dense residential neighborhood. Hovering above the existing plinth of the first-floor volume is a truncated cone, both encompassed and penetrated by the volume of a splayed cube. This vertical configuration maintains only a tenuous dialog with the single-story existing house, and dramatically occupies the space above it: the cylindrical curves reach beyond the cube's limit as if in an embrace of the neighborhood beyond. The intersection of theses two systems creates voids of natural light and ventilation, as well as ludic details like irregularly shaped windows.

SIPEKI BALÁS VILLA, 1905

Budapest, Hungary

ÖDÖN LECHNER

Ödön Lechner was Budapest's leading Secession architect. He is regarded as the creator of the Hungarian national style, designing the Museum of Applied Arts (1896) and numerous other public buildings. Béla Sipeki Balá, a chief lieutenant, commissioned the architect to design this villa nearby Városliget park. The house's facade is typically asymmetrical, highly ornamented, and exotically shaped. A glass-covered conservatory bulges out from the pink-stuccoed facade. A belvedere in a turret, galleries, and porches play with the relationship between indoors and out. Inside, the house was equally grand and eccentric, with iridescent Zsolnay ceramics on the balustrade of the great staircase. In 1944 it was given to the Hungarian Federation of the Blind and Partially Sighted, and it is now the federation's headquarters.

PODDAR RESIDENCE, 1997

Delhi, India

INNI CHATTERJEE & SAMIIR WHEATON

Capitalizing on the natural slope of the site, this multilevel family home opens onto light-filled interior spaces. A wavelike copper-clad roof dramatically crowns the design and is set atop a broad cantilever. Terraced levels, patios, and interlinking corridors are reminiscent of the imperial Mughal palace and courtyard gardens at Fatehpur Sikri. The large interior courtyard pool is showcased on the ground floor and viewed through walls of plate glass from the surrounding rooms. Thin, decorative grit-wash and cement bands punctuate the exterior greystone brick and concrete blocks. These striated surfaces accentuate the elegant horizontal spread of the home. In this house, we see the synthesis of new building materials and postmodern design elements with India's imperial Hindu and Mughal stone palace architectural traditions.

RED HILL, 2008

Red Hill, Victoria, Australia

INARC ARCHITECTS

Red Hill is a small rural town known for its wine, food, and garden produce on the Mornington Peninsula, 53 miles (85 kilometers) south of Melbourne. With views of Port Phillip Bay and passing ships, this retreat is in a beautiful location, nestled within a pine-edged field. Low-profile, hugging the hillside, the house's form is kinked and irregular, which allows for views and good daylight in every room. Each individual space emanates radially from a central hub area. Clad in rusted steel, the sculptural form looks as if it has always been part of the red earth landscape. Interiors are minimal but warmly clad in burnt-orange-colored timber. It is a slick and stylish interpretation of the spirit of the Australian weekend retreat, designed to appeal to city dwellers seeking to unwind and escape from urban pressures.

R128, 2000
Stuttgart, Germany

WERNER SOBEK

Like the homes of many architects, which are often laboratories for testing out theories and ideas, German engineer Werner Sobek's own house in Stuttgart is a live-in experiment, particularly in energy efficiency and flexibility. R128 is a straightforward modular steel-framed structure with complex computer controls which maximize environmental benefits; faucets, doors, and lights, for example, are activated by touchless radar sensors and voice controls—there are no light switches or door handles. Built in just eleven weeks, in theory, the structure could be easily dismantled for recycling or reassembly elsewhere. The home's transparent enclosure is triple glazed, and electricity is supplied by solar panels on the roof; it has no need for additional sources of energy. The house is entered on the top level via a bridge.

SHADOWCLIFF, 1969

Ellison Bay, Wisconsin, USA

HARRY WEESE

The public and private buildings of Weese have made an indelible mark on Chicago and the rest of the Midwestern landscape, but he retains a relatively low profile within the Modernist architectural canon. Shadowcliff is a simple glass box, jutting out across Lake Michigan, improbably hanging from Corten steel beams driven far into a woody hillside. It was built for a businessman who seemingly had no problem with vertigo: in addition to its vertiginous position, there is a porthole window cut in the floor. This and the decorative beams, punched through with hexagons, add a sly note of humor. The Weese oeuvre is mainly one of brick, concrete, and timber, and these material sympathies led him to be labeled an alternative to the more "mainstream" Modernism typified by Mies van der Rohe, Skidmore, Owings & Merrill, and C.F. Murphy Associates.

DIEGO RIVERA AND FRIDA KAHLO HOUSE AND STUDIO, 1932

Mexico City, Mexico

JUAN O'GORMAN

Later in his life, O'Gorman turned away from his early enthusiasm for Le Corbusier's Modernism—his own house, built some twenty-five years after this one, is a sequence of mosaic- and relief-encrusted, cavelike spaces. But here, at the house and studio he built for his friends, the artists Diego Rivera and Frida Kahlo, the abstractions of Le Corbusier's early houses are precisely re-expressed. If anything, O'Gorman's expressed functionalism is even more ideological here; the concrete frame is more powerfully stated than in Le Corbusier's otherwise very similar Ozenfant Studio of 1923, for example. Indeed, ideological commitment seems to have led to O'Gorman's departure from architecture for more than ten years, and to the very different architectural concerns of his later practice, where his work as a painter led to a more local and personal expression.

HAGERTY HOUSE, 1938

Cohasset, Massachusetts, USA

WALTER GROPIUS & MARCEL BREUER

In 1937, having fled Nazi Germany to England, Walter Gropius then accepted a teaching post at Harvard University in the United States. There he met John Hagerty, then a student, who commissioned him to design a house for his mother on a spectacular site overlooking the ocean. Designed by Gropius and Marcel Breuer, who was a former colleague at the Bauhaus and subsequently also at Harvard, the project brought the International Style to the East Coast of America. It features clean, cuboid lines and concrete, and it has exposed radiators and exterior staircases made from welded and galvanized steel pipes. Yet it also uses more traditional New England materials— local stone and wood. Hagerty admitted that friends thought the house "looked like the ladies' wing at Alcatraz or a fruit crate which had washed up on the beach."

KONIECZNY'S ARK, 2015

Kraków, Poland

ROBERT KONIECZNY

Konieczny and his wife's dream was to build a weekend home on a steep hillside plot near Kraków that would be a frame for the landscape. Konieczny wanted a single story, but his wife wanted two. In an elegant marital compromise, he designed a one-level, arklike dwelling—including a "keel" underneath which mirrors the roof's traditional barnlike shape—with just one corner touching the slope, thus elevating the rest of the house into a kind of second floor. The undercut walls also deter any potential intruders, and access is only given by a minidrawbridge. When this and the sliding concrete facades shut, the house becomes a secure concrete box; complicated details and finishes are done away with. Local sheep, horses, and even foxes seem to enjoy sheltering near the house, making it an ark in more ways than one.

MOONLIGHT CABIN, 2014

Melbourne, Victoria, Australia

JACKSON CLEMENTS BURROWS

On a steep, windy hillside above a vast expanse of ocean, this house experiments with the idea of how much space we actually need to live well. Only 646 square feet (60 square meters), the simple orthogonal volume, featuring a spotted gum rainscreen, accommodates a small family with a kitchen, bathroom, living area, and bedrooms in a central pod, opening up the surrounding corridor as a usable space. Jackson Clements Burrows use light and color to bring a lyrical quality to their work: this can be seen here in the wooden folding louver screens—which enable cross ventilation and adaptability—perforated with a circular pattern. By day the screens cast soft shadows; by night they scatter golden medallions of illumination in the darkness. Moonlight Cabin also sustainably harvests rainwater.

PILOTIS IN A FOREST, 2010

Tsumagoi, Gunma, Japan

GO HASEGAWA

In a forest northwest of Tokyo, this aerial nest is lifted up on slim steel pilotis 21 feet (6.5 meters) above the ground. This is just the right height to get shading from foliage in the summer, and views of Mount Asama in winter when the mature trees have shed their leaves. The space under the house serves as a comfortable, cool patio area furnished with hammocks for lounging. Portions of the floor and ceiling are louvered, to further integrate the sights and sounds of the forest. The commission came from a couple in their sixties who wanted a forest retreat. Hasegawa is particularly interested in spaces that he calls "slightly outdoor," aiming to dissolve the boundaries between different spaces—house and forest, inside and outside. Stilt homes are common in this marshy area, but this project literally takes the concept to a higher level.

KONING EIZENBERG HOUSE, 1993

Santa Monica, California, USA

KONING EIZENBERG

The end facade of this long, skinny house—2,700 square feet (250 square meters) but measuring only 17 feet (5 meters) wide—reveals its designers' biggest concerns: blurring the boundaries between indoors and outside, and playing with transitional elements, such as doors and windows. This Santa Monica house—designed by Australian-born, Los Angeles-based architects, Hank Koning and Julie Eizenberg, for themselves and their family—boasts oversized, ground-floor doors that slide open to seamlessly connect house (specifically the living room) and garden. The diagonally patterned, green stucco skin fulfills the designers' intention to conceal the house amid the surrounding landscape. In the end, the architecture becomes merely a backdrop to the outdoors—the epitome of informal living popularized in both southern California and Australia.

POLI HOUSE, 2005
Coliumo, Chile

PEZO VON ELLRICHSHAUSEN

On Chile's Coliumo Peninsula, overlooking the Pacific Ocean, this project is set atop a rocky outcrop. The Poli House encompasses a small cultural center with exhibition space and temporary summer lodgings that accommodate the program of artists-in-residence at the center. The design needed to balance two counterpoised qualities: a monumental public building and the privacy of a domestic setting. To solve this, the structure's cubic form is framed by deep walls that act as cavities to hide away domestic elements, such as a kitchen and wardrobes. This gives each room the freedom to be used for a variety of functions—from sleeping and dining to creating artworks. Due to its remote setting, the entire project is constructed with concrete set in untreated formwork. The slats of its horizontal strata display the history of the project's construction.

EL RAY, 2008
Kent, England, UK

SIMON CONDER ASSOCIATES

Located on the tip of a wind blasted peninsula in Kent, Dungeness is home to a variety of shacks, tarred fisherman's huts, and modern beach houses. The late filmmaker Derek Jarman had a cottage here, with an artsy garden; the otherworldly landscape is largely a shingle expanse dotted with sea kale and Nottingham catchfly, and brooding sea. This home was built around an existing nineteenth-century railway passenger car, which was a family's seaside hideaway. The new two-bedroom house features a bell-shaped plan; the straight facade facing the sea. Internal courtyards offer wind-sheltered spots to enjoy the sun on warm days, and above is a roof deck with a 360-degree view of sea and salt marsh. Slot windows provide strategic vistas of a lighthouse and the Dungeness nuclear power station, which looms over the windswept terrain.

SWISSHOUSE XXXII ROSSA, 2017

Rossa, Switzerland

DANIEL BUREN, DAVIDE MACULLO, & MARIO CRISTIANI

Sited in the picturesque Calanca Valley in the Swiss Alps, this house is a collaboration between architect Davide Macullo, whose grandfather is from the village, French conceptual artist Daniel Buren, and Mario Cristiani of Galleria Continua in Italy. Buren's signature stripe motif adorns the timber frame: the green echoes the grass of the valley floor, and pink references the color of the sky during summer sunsets and the wildflowers that grow here. The vertical white stripes on the colorful cladding are formed from slats; they are an integral part of the building, and thus the art is intrinsic to the architecture. Macullo sought to reinterpret the archetype of the house; in vertical projection the Swisshouse forms a cross, and the rounding of its edges and the simple torsion of the roof give it a sense of dynamism.

GWATHMEY HOUSE AND STUDIO, 1967

Amagansett, New York, USA

CHARLES GWATHMEY

Sited in a former potato field, this house and artist's studio were intended to appear sculpted, as though carved out of a solid block of wood. Gwathmey, a leading Modernist and one of the New York Five, began work on the larger of the two structures, the house itself, in 1965, and completed the studio in 1967. The clients were his parents, a painter and a photographer, who commissioned their son just after he left his apprenticeship with Edward Larrabee Barnes. The interiors echo the geometries of the exterior: a workroom and guest bedrooms on the ground floor, and an external staircase leading up to a double-height living room on the first floor, with kitchen and dining spaces. The studio block is positioned at an angle to the main house; the design intent was to create a sense of movement between the two.

WESTON HAVENS HOUSE, 1941

San Francisco, California, USA

HARWELL HAMILTON HARRIS

This home has been compared to Frank Lloyd Wright's Fallingwater (1939) for its imaginative response to a site. But what's critical about this house is the experience of approaching and being in it, rather than its external form. It consists of two volumes—the upper containing a garage and maid's quarters, the lower consisting of three stacked, inverted triangular trusses, supporting the roof and the main and lower floors. They are connected by a high-sided bridge obscuring the house. When visitors enter the living space, they are welcomed by the sight of the ceiling sweeping upward, opening up a surprise 180-degree view of the San Francisco Bay. Harris was a plan-driven architect, but for this site he had to think sectionally. Weston Havens House was the high point of his career and a critically important work of Californian Modernism.

CURTAIN WALL HOUSE, 1995

Itabashi, Tokyo, Japan

SHIGERU BAN

Shigeru Ban's designs express his exploration of the use of various materials in construction (particularly recycled cardboard tubes) to reveal the alternative character of the site and the building. Built in a traditional district of Tokyo, this steel-structured house opens up to its neighborhood in an extraordinary manner. The first-floor deck extends on two elevations, and is mirrored by the roof slab above, from which are suspended double-height fabric curtains. According to Ban, the curtains soften the daylight and, with internal sliding doors, insulate the interior space from the cool night air, especially in winter. The curtains not only create a space that obscures the boundary between inside and out, but also they allow a connection between the open atmosphere of Shitamachi (old downtown) and the interior of the house.

DR EMODI HOUSE, 1969

Tel Aviv, Israel

ISRAEL LOTHAN

Polish-born Lothan moved to Israel in 1935 and enrolled at the Technion-Israel Institute of Technology, where he soon became an important figure, contributing to the development of the country's Modernist movement. Among his many impressive public projects, the Dr Emodi House is one of his most successful implementations of concrete in a private dwelling. Featuring a combination of exposed concrete and raw, white-colored granular plaster, the design of the house combines a traditional Mediterranean building aesthetic with bold, modern forms. The building is protected from the strong sun with a substantial layer of concrete and plaster and has only a few small windows and an enclosed terrace through which to enter the outside world. The house contains three levels inside, with a double-height dining room and an artist's studio at the top of the building.

MARTA PAN AND ANDRÉ WOGENSCKY'S HOUSE-STUDIO, 1952

Dessau, Germany

ANDRÉ WOGENSCKY

This house for the sculptor Marta Pan and her architect husband André Wogenscky is proportioned according to Le Corbusier's Le Modulor; the house circulation spirals from the ground-floor entrance up to the rooftop terrace, where a high parapet surrounds sculpted concrete walls. Rather than defining rooms separately, Wogenscky conceived of the house as a large interior volume, with high ceilings in the living room and workshop, and lower ceilings in bedrooms. A distinctive projecting frame of raw concrete on the southern face creates a brise-soleil for the living room below it. Accents of black, red, and white reflect Wogenscky's fascination with color. An overhaul in the 1970s added a conversation pit and Pan's original kitchen furniture has been replaced. The house is now the Fondation Marta Pan–André Wogenscky.

RUSTIC CANYON KAPPE COLONY, 1967

Los Angeles, California, USA

RAY KAPPE

Ray Kappe created a rich body of architectural work in Southern California. The most extensive collection of Kappe buildings is located in Los Angeles' Rustic Canyon, including post-and-beam cedar cabins and multi-level timber and glass homes. Kappe's own home is also here; that building, sited steeply uphill from the street, bridges over not just the canyonesque hillside, but also a spring-fed creek. Laminated-fir support beams span six concrete towers; inside, lofty areas are staggered around a double-height living room, with view corridors connecting much of the entire space. An extensive use of glazing gives the home the feel of a tree house in the woods. Kappe's architecture provides a sensual combination of building and nature, maximizing both in a way that few architects have been able to do.

VIPP SHELTER, 2014

Copenhagen, Denmark

VIPP

Vipp was founded in 1939 by Holger Nielsen, who established his business with just one metal lathe, producing cutting-edge and stylish domestic products made of steel. Vipp turned its knowledge of metal and understanding of sleek design to this project, a cabin surrounded by ferns, trees, rocks, and grasses. Situated just north of Copenhagen, the shelter is supported by stilts and has an entirely glazed facade overlooking the serene lake nearby. The black steel interior and exterior, pocked with rivets, and the house's form—with a pair of projections like conning towers serving as skylights—are suggestive of a submarine, ready to take the plunge. The interiors are entirely conceived by Vipp, from the kitchen and bath modules to lamps and the ladder to the mezzanine. Prefabricated versions can be purchased.

CASA MOLEDO, 1998
Caminha, Portugal

EDUARDO SOUTO DE MOURA

Architectural critics have identified a "School of Oporto"—which includes Souto de Moura and Álvaro Siza among others—united in a non-doctrinaire response to the complexities of a country in a sometimes difficult transition from its agricultural past. Here, granite walls, like those of the surrounding vineyards of northern Portugal, step up the hillside to form a series of flat terraces. Where the walls become higher, they split to reveal a simple house form—comprising a single row of rooms, glazed both front and back. The topmost terrace is a flat roof that appears almost to float above the live rock of the hillside. The Casa Moledo demonstrates a theme common in Souto de Moura's buildings: the fusion of traditional and modern, of using vernacular architecture without resorting to artifice. The simplest possible means are used, with the richest possible results.

E/C HOUSE, 2014

Pico Island, Portugal

SAMI-ARQUITECTOS

This house on the volcanic island of Pico in the Azores is built inside the ruin of a basalt cottage. Rather than demolishing or renovating the older structure, or integrating it into parts of the new concrete building, the architects made the new house a contemporary echo of the crumbling shell. Some of the inner structure's openings misalign with those of the outer wall, so new window frames older window, which frames the view beyond, creating a fascinating interplay between concrete and basalt, present and past. Rooms open out onto terraces both within the ruin's boundary and beyond it. All these elements—as well as the proximity to an untamed volcanic landscape—combine to give E/C House, intended as a space for contemplation, a powerful sense of time and place.

HOUSE OF TOMORROW, 1960

Palm Springs, California, USA

PALMER & KRISEL

Built for the property developer Bob Alexander and his family, this futuristic three-floor home consists of four circular floating pavilions under a boomerang-shaped roof, reminiscent of the profile of an airplane, and fronted by a cascading water feature. It was used as the honeymoon hideaway for Elvis and Priscilla Presley. Electronics were state of the art, controlling indoor and outdoor temperature, lighting, and irrigation. Palmer & Krisel built more than twenty thousand homes in Southern California, many of which, including the House of Tomorrow, were part of the burgeoning "tract home" industry—houses of similar design on a tract of land. The House of Tomorrow is an embodiment of the earnest optimism and unabashed technological obsession of the time.

NEUGEBAUER HOUSE, 1998

Naples, Florida, USA

RICHARD MEIER

Built in Meier's signature white-and-glass palette, this house faces southwest over Doubloon Bay in a beautiful palm-fringed location. Its concrete-frame-and-masonry structure is clad by limestone slabs. The architectural language borrows from Le Corbusier—the cantilevering, upward-swooshing roof, the freestanding cylindrical garage, and the huge expanses of white. Meier made the public, entry side effectively "closed down," while the private side opens up and looks out over the water. Local planning regulations for the high-prestige neighborhood required "a one in twelve sloping roof." Meier daringly came up with a spectacular steel-framed butterfly structure cantilevering off paired stanchions at 15-foot (4.6-meter) intervals—not quite what the authorities had in mind. Following this, they rewrote the planning code.

VILLA GLASHÜTTE, 1988

Utscheid, Germany

OSWALD MATHIAS UNGERS

Ungers was synonymous with a radical Neo-Rationalism in German architecture that resisted the contemporary avant-garde. Born in 1926, he was one of the most important architects involved with the reconstruction of Berlin, both before and after the fall of the Wall. His work is typified by a devotion to square and cubic forms, and has a stripped-back aesthetic, which verges on austere. With this private residence in Utscheid, Ungers adopts a Palladian approach of symmetry and simplicity. Sited amid a verdant green landscape, the white cube is near ascetic in its blankness, and each facade of the house is identical. All ornament has been forgone, however it still reads as a classical building. The rooms inside are arranged around a central hall and staircase. Villa Glashütte speaks of something new and different but also timeless.

MEMU MEADOWS EXPERIMENTAL HOUSE, 2011

Taiki, Hokkaido, Japan

KENGO KUMA & ASSOCIATES

This experimental house is located in Memu Meadows, a building materials and architectural test site in Hokkaido. The design was inspired by the *chise*, the traditional dwelling of the Ainu, the local indigenous people. A *chise* is covered in bamboo or sedge grass for insulation, and a fire burns all year inside, radiating heat into the earth and keeping the house warm. Kengo Kuma's version has a larch frame stuffed with polyester insulation made from recycled plastic bottles. The cladding is polycarbonate, and the interior membrane is fiberglass sheeting. Instead of a fire in the ground, underfloor hot-water pipes with geothermal heat storage circulate warmth in between the membranes, keeping the house snug in Hokkaido's deeply cold winters. In the summer, daylight is the main light source, flooding through the translucent walls at dawn.

FREY HOUSE II, 1964

Palm Springs, California, USA

ALBERT FREY

"When I saw the landscape of the desert, I knew I found a place I could call home," Albert Frey said to his biographer in 1990. This eyrielike house, in a site dug out from the rocky cliffs of Mount San Jacinto, has panoramic views out over the Coachella Valley. Frey spent five years surveying the site for the house, tracking the movement of the sun. Known for his Desert Modernism style, the architect employed modest materials such as breeze blocks, concrete, corrugated steel, and glass, and seemed to revel in the contrast between High-Tech and nature; a large rock protruding from the cliff face acts as a divider between the living room and bedroom, and features its own integrated light switch. All of the interior details are built in, including sofas, a record player, and a pencil sharpener.

FATHER'S HOUSE, 2003

Xi'an, Shaanxi, China

MADA S.P.A.M

This residence was designed by Qingyun Ma—one of China's best known architects—for his father, and it is located in the Jade Valley, beneath the Qinling mountain range. Ma began the project in 1992; it took eleven years. He hired twenty villagers to collect thousands of stones from nearby creeks, which were carefully arranged by size, shape, and color, and set within a minimal concrete framework forming the house's primary structure. The interior, a collection of sparse and open spaces that provide simple circulation, is lined in plywood with an intricately patterned bamboo veneer, evoking a traditional Chinese domestic atmosphere. Both the ground-floor living area and the second level are faced on one side with floor-to-ceiling glass panels that open out to a courtyard with a reflective pool; the veneer shutters offer privacy.

HANSHA REFLECTION HOUSE, 2011

Nagoya, Aichi, Japan

STUDIO SKLIM

Hansha Reflection House is sited near the entrance to the verdant Misakimizube Koen, a park known for its Japanese cherry trees. The property's magnificent vistas guided the floor plan of this home, which is designed to facilitate reflection both metaphorically and literally. Communal spaces, including the living and dining rooms, are situated on the upper level in an oversized, jutting cantilever. The structure's black outer skin is composed of Galvalume paneling (a galvanized aluminum zinc alloy), and has a matt finish. The slanted, polished stainless-steel panels of the front facade mirror the surroundings and shine with reflected light, particularly at sunset. Essentially a rectangular volume, the residence circulates around an interior courtyard which acts as a ventilation source during the warmer months. A roof-deck provides picturesque views.

DIRTY HOUSE, 2002
London, England, UK

ADJAYE ASSOCIATES

Shoreditch, East London, in the early 2000s was unfashionable and run-down, unlike now. Artists Sue Webster and Tim Noble bought a former furniture warehouse, situated on a side street, for conversion by architect David Adjaye. The couple wanted a clear delineation between home and work: the gutted building was therefore converted into two double-height studios downstairs, with their home above. The building is painted concrete and brick, which distinguishes it from the surrounding redbrick buildings and signals the private activity within; it is also a practical way to mitigate graffiti. The majority of the openings in the old building were reused, and there is a new internal steel structure. On the top floor, there is a roof terrace and parapet. Dirty House became a local landmark and a seminal work for Adjaye.

VILLA EDEN, 2015

Lake Garda, Italy

DAVID CHIPPERFIELD

Overlooking the resort town of Gardone Riviera, Villa Eden is one of a pair of houses in a similar style, which are in turn part of a bigger development involving four architectural practices. David Chipperfield based the design of Villa Eden on Lake Garda's *limonaie* (lemon houses), traditional structures with rows of stone columns, which, along with wooden poles, form a framework for growing lemons on the western shores of the lake. A few of these can still be seen. The villa is constructed of three walls of local stone, while the main elevation overlooking the lake is fully glazed. A pergola of slender concrete columns provides shading over the terrace and creates an inviting outdoor space. The columns' verticality complements the rhythm of the surrounding cypress trees and olive groves.

VILLA NOAILLES, 1932

Hyères, France

ROBERT MALLET-STEVENS

Rendered in unadorned stucco, the street facade of this sprawling villa expresses a monumentality that is not compromised by the playful composition of its geometrical volumes and bold windows. A massive facade hides a luxurious retreat with landscaped terrace gardens, a covered swimming pool, and squash courts. The original project, a five-bedroom weekend home for film enthusiast and art collector Viscount Charles de Noailles, was expanded to eventually include more than sixty rooms, some of which were designed by other architects, including a flower room by Theo van Doesburg and an open-air room by Pierre Chareau. The client originally intended to commission Mies van der Rohe or Le Corbusier for this project, but settled on the untested Mallet-Stevens, whose reputation at the time was based only on inventive movie set designs.

VILLA 1, 2007

Veluwezoom, The Netherlands

POWERHOUSE COMPANY

Located within the Veluwezoom National Park, this house nestles inside a manmade woody grove. To maximize space while meeting local regulations on height and volume, it is laid out over two floors of equal size—one above ground, one below. The inversion derives from placing the public rooms over the private, making a creative distinction between rooms for day and those for night. On the upper level, a concealed steel frame supports the completely glazed envelope. There are eclectic elements: a bookcase in the north wing doubles as a truss, and space is only loosely partitioned. By contrast, the lower floor is sculpted out of cast concrete, with vaulted ceilings and thick walls creating an intimate riposte to the openness above. The Y-shaped plan aims to maximize the sunlight as it makes its way through the grove.

VILLA KOGELHOF, 2013

Noord-Beveland, The Netherlands

PAUL DE RUITER ARCHITECTS

This plot was bought as part of the Dutch ecological estate, Farm Kogelhof, and the client complied with the site's agricultural remit, planting 70,000 trees and establishing a large pond. In concert with its ecological principles, he wanted a highly sustainable home from which to survey the natural surroundings. The T-shaped plan comprises a long glazed volume, balanced above a submerged cubic podium, and supported by a V-shaped column. The architects designed an interior free from typical domestic details: elements such as wardrobes, garaging, and storage are hidden in the lower wing, leaving the upper level a pristine place for contemplation. The house's climatic facade channels heat away in warm months and later releases it from the biomass in cool seasons. Paired with solar and wind energy, this means the house is entirely self-sufficient.

JULES BRADY RESIDENCE, 1970

Long Beach, California, USA

KILLINGSWORTH, BRADY
& ASSOCIATES

The Southern Californian Modernists Edward Killingsworth, Jules Brady, and Waugh Smith graduated from architecture school in 1940, meeting at the Long Beach practice of Kenneth S. Wing. In 1953 they set up their own company, which was driven mainly by Killingsworth's designs, characteristically post-and-beam, with dramatic entrances, flat roofs, open plans, and extensive glazing. The influence of their Case Study House No. 25 (1965) can be seen in the Jules Brady Residence. The monumental 17-foot (5-meter) entrance of this house bisects a facade of translucent glazing, which is enclosed in graceful steel ribs. The first space on entering is a courtyard, which flows into a soaring double-height living room fitted a mezzanine. This is sophisticated indoor-outdoor living that maintains an elegant feel for privacy.

SALT POINT HOUSE, 2008

Salt Point, New York, USA

THOMAS PHIFER AND PARTNERS

This house was built for a New York couple, and is sited in a meadow with a small private lake. Its engineered, High-Tech aesthetic seems, at first view, to be at odds with its natural surroundings. The two-story rectangular box's north and south facades are introverted, with matching uninterrupted ribbon windows; the east and west facades are, conversely, fully glazed with black frames. Double-height space at both ends gives generous height to the interior. The home is cloaked by perforated stainless-steel screens that provide shelter from sun, rain, and wind. They extend horizontally beyond the house to create a sheltered porch, and they rise vertically above the roofline so that the trees beyond appear to merge with the facade. The interiors, including custom furniture and cabinetry, are clad with maple plywood.

BAHIA HOUSE, 1998

Bahia, Brazil

GAETANO PESCE

Bahia House was designed as the vacation home of Gaetano Pesce, the Italian-born architect and industrial designer. Overlooking a bay dotted with giant palm trees, the house is a grouping of six pavilions, all linked, of different styles, each of them as sassy as the next. One is covered in multicolored resin tiles which resemble fish scales, a playful reference to the architect's name; another is made of locally manufactured rubber, which has been infused with lavender to mask the material's scent. The third, pictured here, is a more introverted, cartoonish concrete fort, perched on pillars, with porthole windows. One of the project's key drivers is untamed color. As Pesce has said, "Bahia House is full of color because color is important to transfer a meaning that is very close to the meaning of life."

MALATOR HOUSE, 1994

St Brides Bay, Wales, UK

FUTURE SYSTEMS

The Malator House is all but invisible; only the elliptical glazed facade orientated toward the sea gives away the fact of a human presence. The facade is like a lens, cut into the landscape above the cliffs on the Welsh coastline, trained on the magnificent view west. The rest of the structure, consisting of an arc-shaped retaining wall banked up with earth, and a plywood roof laid on a steel ring-beam, is entirely camouflaged with grass. Inside, an unclosed space is divided by free-standing service pods, which contain the bathroom and kitchen, and is dominated by a large circular sofa. While at Future Systems, Jan Kaplický and Amanda Levete built a reputation on innovation, pushing their designs to aesthetic and technical limits. This house represents a development of the "unique language of curvaceous forms" that characterized most of their work.

STAHL HOUSE, 1960

Los Angeles, California, USA

PIERRE KOENIG

"Los Angeles is their back yard" was how the Los Angeles *Examiner* described the new house, also known as Case Study House No. 22, of the Stahls in 1960. Pierre Koenig's second project for the Case Study House Program is the epitome of the reductivist architecture of the "Contemporary" style of 1950s California. With its expansive roof-deck, overhanging eaves, and shimmering swimming pool, it still features regularly in many fashion and film shoots. Built on a relatively cheap site, due to its poor soil and steeply sloping aspect, the owners wanted to take full advantage of the impressive view. The architect cantilevered the main living space of the steel-frame house way out over the slope on massive reinforced concrete beams supported by huge caissons that are bored into the ground.

INVISIBLE HOUSE, 2012

Blue Mountains, New South Wales, Australia

PETER STUTCHBURY

Tucked into a ridge overlooking the wilderness of Megalong Valley, in the Blue Mountains west of Sydney, this house is neither dwarfed by nor in competition with its setting. The long, low-lying home, barely visible on approach, is designed to look like an extension of the mountain. Its graceful cantilevering roof—designed to act as both a dam and thermal device—is topped with two steel rooftop "boxes" (a light scoop to the north and sleeping eyrie to the south), whose materiality evokes Australian bush life. Composed of robust materials—including concrete, Mudgee stack stone, hoop pine, fine steel, brass, and copper—the home was constructed over three years by a local builder. In 2016 the Invisible House won a RIBA Award for International Excellence.

GARDEN & HOUSE, 2011

Tokyo, Tokyo Prefecture, Japan

RYUE NISHIZAWA

Wedged between two urban apartment blocks, this garden tower-cum-house appears as a series of floating concrete planes. These are held together by three reinforced-concrete columns and a slender steel pole, a design that is perhaps a nod to Le Corbusier's Dom-Ino frame house; a circular cutout in the roof slab presents a Modernist architectural motif that is visible from the street. On a tiny 26 x 13 foot (8 x 4 meter) plot, this is a home that prioritizes plant life as much as people—each floor incorporates a terrace for nurturing vegetation. Crammed into the ground floor are cooking and dining areas, while there are small bedrooms on the second and fourth floors, and the bathroom is on the third floor. In a sense, it is the plants themselves that create the facade, and fine gauze curtains allow for some form of privacy.

HOUSE IN UTSUNOMIYA, 2015

Utsunomiya, Tochigi, Japan

SUPPOSE DESIGN OFFICE

On one side of this tentlike house, the pitched roof swoops right down to the ground, completely covering a graveled terrace and garden area. This not only creates a feeling of safety and enclosure but also eradicates the boundary between indoor and outdoor space. The architects said they wanted to build a home where "a family can have an open-air meal, or use the garden on rainy days, which changes the atmosphere of the daily life inside an ordinary house." It makes living in it more playful—and perhaps sometimes similar to camping. The house is clad in distinctive metal sheeting called Galvalume (a zinc and aluminum alloy). Painted white, it has a glossy, light-reflecting exterior. The interior, lined with pale cedar wood, is similarly bright. Strategically placed cutaways in the roof create terraces and openings to illuminate the house.

CROWLEY HOUSE, 2014

Marfa, Texas, USA

CARLOS JIMÉNEZ STUDIO

The Crowley House rests on a flat hilltop in Marfa overlooking the rolling grass dunes of the Chihuahua Desert. As a Texas native, architect Carlos Jiménez knows the state's topography intimately. Marfa weather features intense afternoon sun and strong winds; materials like concrete, galvanized steel, and wood were chosen to withstand the climate. Large aluminum-framed windows invite views of differing scales into the domestic space, showcasing the intimacy of native flora, and the expansiveness of the chiseled mountain ranges on the horizon. The gentle color palette of earthy grays and warm browns allows the house to blend in easily with nature's textures. Following the light's journey was a consideration in order to create protection—important because of the owner's contemporary art collection—without inducing darkness.

SCHINDLER HOUSE, 1922

Los Angeles, California, USA

RUDOLPH SCHINDLER

The Modernist architect Schindler redefined the contemporary Californian home with this avant-garde residence and studio. This revisionist experiment in communal living was designed for Schindler and his wife, Pauline, and another couple—Marian and Clyde Chace. Each person had his or her own room, to express his or her individuality; there was a shared kitchen and a tranquil patio for each couple. The pinwheel plan allowed for both privacy and communality. Using "slab-tilt" wall construction, the house had a heavy bunkerlike appearance, lightened by extensive glazing. Dark wood frames gave it a Japanese aesthetic typical of early Modernism. The Schindlers hosted Hollywood "salons" at the home, and when they divorced in the 1930s, continued to share—living separately but together.

WEIZMANN HOUSE, 1937

Rehovot, Israel

ERICH MENDELSOHN

Chaim Weizmann was a biochemist who was the head of the Zionist movement for more than thirty years and became first president of the State of Israel in 1949. He lived in this house starting in 1937, and it became the official presidential residence until his death in 1952. Built unusually around a courtyard with swimming pool, which is typically situated in the backyard, it is an early example of Israeli International Style Modernism, which arose as a result of Jewish architects fleeing Nazi Germany—as Mendelsohn had in 1933 (most of his buildings in Germany were destroyed by the Nazis). Despite the house's cutting-edge design, Chaim's wife, Vera, adopted a more traditional interior decor, telling Mendelsohn: "You have built a modern house. It is very lovable and livable … but I cannot live with your interior decoration!"

DO HOUSE, 2001

Los Vilos, Chile

CAZÚ ZEGERS

Do House, located in Los Vilos on the coast of central Chile, is a fortresslike residential villa. Perched on a rocky beach facing the Pacific, it is, on the one hand, defensive—shielding against the potential onslaught of the ocean—and, at the same time, calm and built with a remarkable level of precision. A circular concrete wall—mimicking two protective arms—delineates the boundary of the house, while a bridged pathway from the entrance of the estate bisects the building and points out toward the sea. Inside, essentially every wall surface, soffit, and ceiling is expressed in exposed concrete, while the floor is layered with wood. Two large glazed walls—one facing the sea, the other facing land—flood the tall interior spaces with natural light and offer wide views of the expanded horizon.

SAM AND RUTH VAN SICKLE FORD HOUSE, 1950

Aurora, Illinois, USA

BRUCE GOFF

This tangerine-shaped house in suburban Aurora was the home of civil engineer Albert (Sam) Van Sickle Ford, and his wife, Ruth, an artist and teacher. Bruce Goff, an influential figure of the American organic movement, called circles "an informal, gathering-around friendly form." The house he designed for the couple was described as a "fine spangling lustrous toy" by *Architectural Forum* magazine, and is structured with Quonset hut ribs, similar to those of the Nissen hut. Comprising a primary dome with two semicircular bedroom wings, the house has a base wall constructed of cannel coal, made weatherproof and smudge-proof, inset with marbles and waste glass for sparkle. Growing tired of critical onlookers gawking at the house, the Fords put up a sign outside saying, "We don't like your house either."

Y-HOUSE, 1999

Catskills, New York, USA

STEVEN HOLL

This weekend retreat is sited on a hilltop in a remote section of the Catskill Mountains. The roof of the house slopes continuously upward, beginning at the one-story entry on the north, before branching or forking into a Y-shape at its center, terminating in two-story volumes, each with large balconies projecting toward the south. The iron-oxide red-colored steel roof folds down in triangular sections, and the red-stained horizontal cedar siding of the walls bends inward. In the branching plan of this house, Holl engages Frank Lloyd Wright's ideal of each primary room being opened to sunlight and views on three sides. The client, a European family with a collection of modern art, benefit from the house's split form, which allows more wall space for hanging their sizable collection.

SHAM LAL HOUSE, 1975

New Delhi, India

RAJ REWAL

Brickwork infuses this house with a complex texture. Raj Rewal's attention to detail and sensitivity to material are evident in the brick *jali* (lattice or screen work), which act as parapets for roof terraces, and the formwork marks left exposed on the balcony ceilings. Vertical emphasis disappears in the fastidiously cornered brickwork, favouring the horizontality of the land. Brick-on-edge cornices, plastered fascias and an unobtrusive transition from floor to flora are gestures that reconcile house and garden. These finer details explain why such functionalism in brick was popular among Rewal's generation. Inspired by Jeanneret's Chandigarh and Le Corbusier's Primitivist oeuvre, this fresh aesthetic happily marries Enlightenment-style Rationalism with India's labour-intensive building technologies.

VILLA NORRKÖPING, 1964

Norrköping, Sweden

SVERRE FEHN

This residence was designed as part of a competition for Danish, Finnish, and Swedish architects under the theme "Nordic Villa Park." Entries had to be able to accommodate a small family, and follow modular construction principles. The house has a floor plan that follows a Greek cross shape, with four identical facades; kitchen and bathroom are located in the center of its cross, while the living area, with movable panels to configure the space appropriately, inhabited the cross's "arms." Villa Norrköping has been described as being influenced by Andrea Palladio's Villa La Rotonda in the Veneto; in reality, Fehn was likely more influenced by Le Corbusier's *promenade architecturale*—although contrary to the Corbusian promenade, in Fehn's structure the movement is circular, with no definite start and end.

4X4 HOUSE, 2003

Kobe, Hyogo, Japan

TADAO ANDO ARCHITECT & ASSOCIATES

This beachside house, bordered on the north by a two-lane highway and to the south by the Inland Sea, is close to the epicenter of the 1995 Great Hanshin Earthquake that devastated Kobe. Ando wanted the house to be a sort of memorial to the disaster. Taking advantage of the seascape but turning its back on the traffic, he designed four stacking cubes. The topmost level cantilevers sideways and outward to create more room, yet it is also symbolic of displacement. Ando's signature material, concrete, is studded by the anchor points of its wooden molds, and gives the building a feeling of security. Another client later asked Ando for the same house on a neighboring plot. With this commission, the architect could complete his original idea of two houses, though without the communication between them that he had earlier conceptualized.

KRIER HOUSE, 1987

Seaside, Florida, USA

LEON KRIER

In a town of towers, this house stands tallest. Krier—a leading proponent of the 1980s New Urbanist movement to return to traditional towns and architecture—was an advisor in the early stages of planning Seaside, the famous new resort community in the Florida Panhandle. He decided to build a house of his own there which has become a landmark in more ways than one. It is a small house on a compact site, but rises high in the air to its "temple" top that affords a fine view of the Gulf of Mexico. By regulation, all Seaside houses have white picket fences, and this one is no exception. Krier has spent most of his career in the theoretical realm of architecture, writing, and drawing, and this house is his first built work. It is a craftsman's house, intricately assembled as if built by a ship's carpenter. It was extended in 2003.

DELTA SHELTER, 2002

Mazama, Washington, USA

OLSON KUNDIG

Rising geometrically from a field in a floodplain next to the Methow River, in rural Washington State, the Delta Shelter is a small cabin for weekend use. It is clad in double-height steel panels, and can be completely shuttered up when the owners are away. But more than that, it is completely weatherproof. Cranking a wheel slides the steel shutters over the glazed parts of the facade in a refreshingly low-tech way. In this respect, it is a house with a dual personality— generously open in the warm months and protectively closed when the temperature cools. Cantilevered steel decks extend from the top and middle levels and provide space for outdoor sleeping and entertaining. The weathered steel, with its warm, earthlike coloring, has the appearance of bark, and helps the house blend in with the wooded grove surrounding it.

RING HOUSE, 2006

Karuizawa, Nagano, Japan

MAKOTO TAKEI & CHIE NABESHIMA/TNA

Karuizawa, a peaceful resort town in the mountains near Nagano, is a retreat for city dwellers. The position of the house was influenced by factors including coding guidelines and boundary issues but principally by the delicate ecology of the landscape. The building assumes a slender, vertical profile on a compact footprint. With a partially sunken basement level, it is laid out over three stories plus roof terrace but this is not easily read from outside. Each elevation is identical, articulated in contrasting bands of cedar and glass that wrap round the ramin wood frame. Floor slabs are hidden behind the solid planes, as are bespoke functional elements like the kitchen counter and stove. The overall effect is of a single composition, with no discernible front or back. Views through the structure preserve the character of the existing forest.

NESTLED BOX, 2006

Chofu, Tokyo, Japan

MILLIGRAM ARCHITECTURAL STUDIO

This family home and workspace is constructed mainly from wood, and the building is configured as a series of boxes within the outer shell. A corridor between the interior wall and the nested cubes allows movement to circulate freely, while a large atrium at the heart of the house visually connects all its different parts. Cascading plants and brightly colored, oversized hanging tapestries fill the central void, creating an interior that emanates warmth and has a charming lived-in quality. On the facade, planks of warm-hued wood, positioned in alternating directions, appear woven together in a checkerboard pattern; within it are a multitude of square and rectangular openings that permit natural light inside. Throughout, rooms are built like a loft, with full-height walls only enclosing the private functions of the home.

PAPER HOUSE, 1995

Lake Yamanaka, Yamanashi, Japan

SHIGERU BAN

The Paper House, which overlooks a lake with Mount Fuji towering in the distance, represents the first authorized use of paper tubes as a structural material in a permanent building. Designing with the explicit purpose of introducing tubes into Japanese building regulations, Ban created a dramatic showcase for this structural material. An S-shaped arrangement of 108 tubes, of which nine provide vertical structural support (the remaining support lateral forces), is imposed on a square floorplan, and creates a series of multifunctional interior and exterior spaces. Each tube is screwed to cruciform wooden joints in the column bases. Narrow slots between the tubes allow light to enter the living area and allow for a partial view inside or outside. A horizontal roofline and vertical columns underscore the house's structural purity.

DOUBLE CHIMNEY, 2008

Karuizawa, Nagano, Japan

ATELIER BOW-WOW

Atelier Bow-Wow is Momoyo Kaijima and Yoshiharu Tsukamoto—their studio was established in 1992. They call their design concept "behaviorology," which is centered on the various behaviors of three things: natural elements, human beings, and a building itself. Known for their quirky humor, Bow-Wow's architectural plans include unconventional details, including "flower pots, cats, coffee cups, and slippers under the bed," said Tskukamoto. Tucked into a woodland clearing, this typically curious home seems familiar yet strangely unfamiliar. An archetypal house form has been split and released outward, creating a home on hinges. One side is for guests, the other for its owners. Double Chimney is positioned carefully among the trees, opening itself up to the southern light. Since the house is sliced in two, more warmth and air find their way inside.

HOUSE VI, 1918

Bergen, The Netherlands

MARGARET KROPHOLLER

House VI—a masonry house with a sculpted, thatched roof—was one of seventeen country houses built in the artists' colony of Park Meerwijk, in a verdant coastal town in northern Holland. One of the first realized Dutch Expressionist projects, this colony was supervised by the Amsterdam School architect Jan Frederick Staal with Piet Kramer, G. F. La Croix, C. J. Blaauw and Margaret Kropholler—Staal's young assistant who later became his second wife, and the architect of House VI. Meezennest (Tom-Tit's Nest) is in fact a double house, with its mirror image, Meerlhuis (Blackbird House) on the opposite side. As one of the most evocative schemes in the colony, this house draws from a combination of Japanese, Indonesian, and Dutch vernacular sources, as well as the ideals of the English Arts and Crafts movement.

GLASS HOUSE, 1949

New Canaan, Connecticut, USA

PHILIP JOHNSON

This house, small in scale yet prodigious in terms of its influence, shows Johnson's indebtedness to the work of Mies van der Rohe: in the use of standard steel sections for a strong yet decorative finish of the facade, in the corner treatment, and the relation of the column to the window frames. It was based on Mies' earlier 1945 sketches for the as yet unbuilt Farnsworth House, and is an iconic work in the International Style. Johnson is working here almost as a landscape designer, treating the house as a frame for its natural environment; he uses the lawn as a well-groomed carpet on which to place the architectural object. The house is externally symmetrical, organized around an interior brick cylinder, which stands in contrast to the incorporeality of the glass envelope. The French architect Auguste Perret, on visiting the house, reportedly remarked, "Too much glass."

THE HIDDEN PAVILION, 2016

Las Rozas, Spain

PENELAS ARCHITECTS

Sited in a forest glade northwest of Madrid, this silvan retreat cantilevers over a small waterfall in the same way as Frank Lloyd Wright's Fallingwater (1939). The architects went to great lengths to protect existing trees and to make them part of the one-bedroom house itself. The rusted steel pavilion is designed around them, allowing the trees to penetrate gaps in the structure. In order to accommodate a two-hundred-year-old holm oak tree, one side of the house was given oblique sides. Five red cylinders on the roof funnel light—which had been blocked by the oak—into the house, giving it a near nautical look. In a lovely symbiosis, the all-glass walls are screened by the trees themselves. The interior has a straightforward material palette of cherrywood finishes and dark flooring. The owners use the retreat for rest and meditation.

BUBBLE PALACE, 1989

Théoule-sur-Mer, France

ANTTI LOVAG

Located in Cannes, Lovag's Palais Bulles—or Bubble Palace—steps down the Estérel Massif like a creeping mat of tapioca. Designed in 1975, it is an example of the Hungarian architect's philosophy of "habitology"—a vague concept that included banning right angles and straight lines. Circles and curves, he thought, were closer to nature and closer, therefore, to the human body. The form of the house was created organically: Lovag first got to know the terrain, creating an iron rebar network without foundations, deciding then on the type of openings. The framework was covered with mesh, concrete, and two layers of fiberglass-reinforced polyester. There is a very similar house by Lovag—his first built project—farther down the slope, called Maison Bernard; it was recently renovated by French architect Odile Decq.

FUTURO HOUSE, 1968

Hiekkaharju, Vantaa, Finland

MATTI SUURONEN

The Futuro House was designed in 1968 as the ideal holiday home, using the ratio of 1:2 to give it its perfect symmetrical and elliptical shape. The UFO-like prefabricated, glass-fiber house could be built by four people in an afternoon and transported to any site by helicopter, with its fully equipped kitchen, bathroom, two bedrooms, and lounge already installed. Some 600 models were made by the plastics factory, Polykem AB of Helsinki, even though its price was too high for mass production. However, its fashionable, space-age design was exhibited around the world and influenced many other types of building developed using the same system of construction, including kiosks, service stations, and hotel complexes. The oil crisis in 1973, however, resulted in the cancelling of an order for more than 15,000 modules.

WALL HOUSE, 2007
Santiago, Chile

FAR FROHN&ROJAS

The architects designed this multifaceted, tentlike home for a retired couple as a series of spaces within enclosing layers. The innermost core is made of concrete: a hidden, introverted "cave" containing two bathrooms. This is surrounded by two bands of wooden shelving, some areas of which are open, some of which are not—porous yet practical. This shelving defines the living space, kitchen, and guest room on the ground floor and a studio on the first. Following this is a "milky shell" of polycarbonate insulating panels that allow in light but protect the house from the strong Chilean sun. Finally, the entire house is wrapped in a soft fabric membrane that adds further insulation and keeps out mosquitoes. Its translucence gives tantalizing glimpses of the multiple layers underneath.

CARING WOOD, 2017

Kent, England, UK

JAMES MACDONALD WRIGHT
& NIALL MAXWELL

Caring Wood is a contemporary vernacular English country house, built for three generations of one family. Its shape was inspired by traditional oast houses, the distinctive hop-drying towers that populate the Kent countryside. Four towers—one for the parents and one for each daughter's family—are positioned in a dynamic pinwheel formation around a central courtyard. The core contains communal spaces, including an area for displaying art and hosting chamber music recitals. The roof is clad with more than 150,000 handmade peg tiles from Sussex. Its sculptural form is expressed internally through soaring ceiling heights, and apertures at each apex provide natural light and ventilation. The home won the RIBA House of the Year award in 2017, and the institution wrote of the house that it balances "the need for grandeur with intimacy."

FACE HOUSE, 1974
Kyoto, Kyoto Prefecture, Japan

KAZUMASA YAMASHITA

A funny, yellow, grinning face suddenly interrupts a row of conventional houses in downtown Kyoto. This home's painted concrete facade is embellished with two rounded windows, a projected cylindrical ventilation opening, and recessed glass entrance doors. It accommodates two studios for a graphic designer at street level, and family living space on the second and top levels. In designing this house, Yamashita applied his "separate parallel plan," in which the residential area is arranged to the south and service space to the north, with a circulation area between them. Playfully treated as a signboard, the front facade of the Face House demonstrates an early postmodern tendency, while the interior arrangement expresses Yamashita's commitment to an alternative living environment.

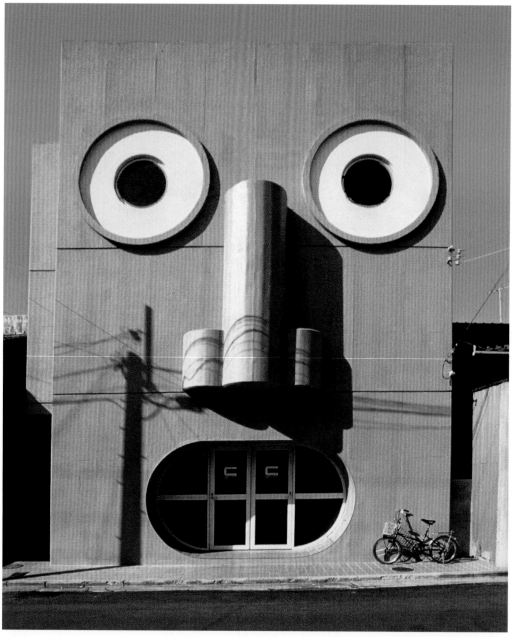

THE THEMATIC HOUSE, 1985

London, England, UK

CHARLES JENCKS
& TERRY FARRELL

Architectural critic Charles Jencks has described the works which he and architect friends (including Terry Farrell and Piers Gough) carried out on his 1840s Holland Park house as an "attempt to face directly the question of meaning" in architecture. The garden elevation can be read as an abstract representation of his family: father, mother, and two children, with their dog at the center. Jencks, who influenced and defined the postmodern movement through works such as *The Language of Post-Modern Architecture* (1977), was interested in exploring the symbolic potential of architecture. The interior of the house is a symbolic expression of time, completely restructured around a new concrete circular staircase, "the sun well," and a two-story "moon well" which has complex iconography incorporating science and philosophy.

CASA CARACOLA , 2011

Guerrero, Mexico

PAUL CREMOUX STUDIO

Casa Caracola (Conch House) is located with the Tres Vidas Golf Course on the Mexican Pacific coast. It consists of four interlocking boxlike volumes with an open-air courtyard at the center of the structure. Each of these four elements projects out in a different direction to make the most of varying views. Each, too, connects with the outdoors in a different way, via a wrapping veranda, deck, balcony, or fully glazed wall. The accommodations include guest rooms and a library on the ground floor; and living and dining rooms, a kitchen, a master bedroom, and an additional guest room on the second floor. The master bedroom, within a huge concrete tube, hovers on two concrete slabs, creating a massive outdoor deck. The cantilevering volumes also provide shading in the typically hot Mexican climate.

HOUSE NA, 2010

Tokyo, Tokyo Prefecture, Japan

SOU FUJIMOTO

This house, in a quiet residential area of Tokyo, resembles open scaffolding or a giant bookcase. It has three notional stories, subdivided into spaces of different heights using no fewer than twenty-one different floor plates. According to Fujimoto, the openness and connectedness of the house make it feel like living in a tree. There is visual and spatial connection from one level to another—it's possible to interact with people on different floors, subverting ideas of what a room's boundaries should be. There is also absolute transparency from outside to inside, although to maintain some privacy, many of the glass walls are covered by screens. Inhabitants can dangle their legs from the totally open upper platforms, an impossibility under planning regulations in many other countries.

KALMAN HOUSE, 1976

Minusio, Switzerland

LUIGI SNOZZI

Kalman House sits above Lake Maggiore in an region dominated by holiday villas, many of which are Neoclassical in style. Neatly set into the hillside, with its rough-cast walls, flat roof, and simple openings, the house is an unobtrusive concrete box. It forms just one part of a carefully planned route that begins by a stream and finishes at a pergola. The retaining wall on the west side extends outward, cutting into the hillside to support a narrow terrace. The southeast corner is cut away, exposing the concrete frame and accommodating a terrace and balcony. Horizontal windows sit high up on the east wall, so that views of the road are limited. The emphasis is on the south facade, which is fully glazed with steel-framed windows. Inside, the rooms are finished in white stucco, with terracotta floors.

VILLA MÜLLER, 1930

Prague, Czech Republic

ADOLF LOOS

In 1928 Frantisek Müller, co-owner of the Kapsa-Müller construction company, commissioned Adolf Loos to build a home for his family overlooking Prague Castle in Stresovice, a wealthy neighborhood of northwest Prague. The cubic, flat-roofed house was a showcase for reinforced concrete, a material that Müller pioneered. The simple facade belies a complex interior spatial plan, where Loos pushed his concept of Raumplan, a perception of architecture as spatial sequences, to its limit. He designed a series of transitioning spaces, at different levels according to function and importance, flowing off a central staircase. This suggested a thoroughly modern mode of bourgeois living. In contrast to the facade, the interior design was lavish. Loos held his sixtieth birthday party here, calling it "my most beautiful house."

CASA DO CINEMA, 2003
Porto, Portugal

EDUARDO SOUTO DE MOURA

Portuguese architect Eduardo Souto de Moura, who won the Pritzker Prize in 2011, is best known for Braga Municipal Stadium (2003) and the red pyramidal towers of the Casa das Histórias Paula Rego (2008) in Cascais. This singular structure, which is defined by two big, periscope-like windows, is Souto de Moura at his most expressive. Built for the film director Manoel de Oliveira, it wryly pretends to be similar to the surrounding houses in the modest neighborhood of Foz, and the distorted volume adapts to the small plot characteristic of the locale. The building's odd trapezoid shape (when viewed from above) and asymmetry bring to mind the work of Álvaro Siza, with whom Souto de Moura collaborated between 1974 and 1979 before he established his own practice.

SAINT-ANGE RESIDENCE, 2015

Seyssins, France

STUDIO ODILE DECQ

Overlooking the city of Grenoble, this blackened volume stands on a tight, narrow site in Seyssins. The house encompasses an artist's home arranged over five floors, the lowest double-height volume partially hunkered into the earth, providing an open-plan space for a studio. Because the site has uninterrupted views south to the distant French Alps, the architects saw an opportunity to maximize this unspoilt panorama. Accordingly, the tower element rises from this compass point and its chamfered, irregular section contains three levels—a living room, a bedroom, and a belvedere at the top which is connected by a spiral staircase. To give coherency to the project's irregular profile, the entire building is constructed from concrete, and its pine cladding is finished with black asphalt. Its receding hue diminishes the effect of the unusual composition.

C3 HOUSE, 2017

Ancón District, Lima Province, Peru

BARCLAY & CROUSSE
ARCHITECTURE

In this area of Peru, where the Andes and the Pacific ocean meet, the climate is humid yet completely free of rain, and its landscape reveals itself to be otherworldly, even Martian. The layout includes four platforms: one for vehicles and services, two sheltering the bedrooms, and another dedicated to social activities. The roof is conceived as a series of concrete vaults which evoke a sense of spaciousness, as if there were no roof at all. This feeling of openness is further enhanced as the living room extends seamlessly to the wood-lined terrace, where an infinity pool is situated to face the ocean. While the interior is kept simple and practical, the exterior exposes an extravagance that stems more from an eloquent collage of subtly unusual geometric shapes than from an opulence of muted materials.

THE DESERT HOUSE, 1993

Joshua Tree National Park, California, USA

KENDRICK BANGS KELLOGG

Kendrick Bangs Kellogg is maybe not the best known talent of the Modern organic style, being overshadowed, for example, by his contemporary John Lautner. Kellogg built this house, sited amid the rounded boulders of Joshua Tree National Park, for artists Bev and Jay Doolittle, who didn't want to disturb the landscape. The house is formed of twenty-six cantilevered concrete columns sunk into the bedrock. The armadillo-like form huddles within the cleft of a rocky hillock to become part of the terrain. Openings in the house are not clearly defined, and occasionally the desert rocks erupt into the interior. Designer John Vugrin executed the detailing, both inside and out. He spent a decade on this, creating harmonious surreal forms, such as a spiked perimeter fence resembling fish bones, and a glass-and-metal table that swoops upward, fusing with the ceiling.

NEW RIVER STUDIO, 1975

New River, Arizona, USA

WILL BRUDER ARCHITECTS

Bruder is a self-trained architect, with a background in sculpture, philosophy, engineering, and art history. For a time he apprenticed with the Italian architect Paolo Soleri, and also trained under the tutelage of Latvian-American Gunmar Birkerts. This house, which juts out from a spiny ridge, is Bruder's own studio and retreat, set in the middle of the desert north of Phoenix. New River Studio is alive with "honest" materials: concrete, corrugated sheet metal, and timber. It sits comfortably in the blistering environment, amid extensive desert vegetation—the weathered sundeck overlooks panoramic stands of saguaro. The interiors are modest and sparely decorated. Since 1974, Bruder has established a reputation for creating architecture which is sensitive to the unusual character of the American desert landscape.

CASA KIKÉ, 2007

Cahuita, Costa Rica

GIANNI BOTSFORD ARCHITECTS

Casa Kiké is an idyllic retreat in Cahuita, a village bordering a national park of white beaches and coral reefs. The dwelling, built for a writer, is made up of two pavilions made entirely of local timber, and constructed using indigenous techniques. The first sits on stilts on concrete pad foundations. In the corrugated-steel-clad, hangarlike structure, roof beams are up to 33 feet (10 meters) long, and there are no supporting columns. Its monopitched roof angles upward toward the seashore, and the end facade is completely glazed and louvered, facilitating good lighting and ventilation. This pavilion is comprised of a daytime studio space with a library and grand piano. Reached by a raised wooden walkway, an identical smaller pavilion is positioned nearby with a bedroom and bathroom.

PEARLROTH HOUSE, 1959

Westhampton Beach, New York, USA

ANDREW GELLER

Built in 1959 for Arthur and Mitch Pearlroth, this beach house, one of several modest, abstract homes designed by Geller, is known as the "Double Diamond." It quickly became an icon of Modernism. Architectural historian Alastair Gordon listed it as one of the "ten best Houses of the Hamptons." Supported on cedar posts and blocks, it is formed of two elongated volumes, both of which are rotated ninety degrees to form a jaunty box kite shape which is clad in copper. The gap between the two units is occupied by a glazed living area; high-peaked ceilings evoke the feeling of an American Indian tent. Now owned by the Pearlroths' son Jonathan, the hut has undergone a complete restoration by the architects CookFox. It serves as a pool house for a new, much larger residence positioned behind it.

SIMPLE HOUSE, 2017

Jeju-si, Jeju Province, South Korea

MOON HOON

On Jeju Island this theatrical dwelling, designed by Moon Hoon, was built as a holiday retreat for a family. They had originally requested a more private, bunkerlike structure, but then had a complete change of mind, wanting something more showy. They certainly got their wish, with Hoon's three stacking reinforced-concrete cuboids fixed together with oblique beams, which give additional bracing against the island's notably windy weather. Featuring numerous verandas, the house offers a range of views across the lush island landscape. The three floors connect via a central staircase. Seoul-based Hoon is known for his playfully adventurous structures which have resembled, among other things, an owl, a hairdryer, and a lollipop. The name Simple House is no doubt intended to be tongue in cheek.

LOVELL HEALTH HOUSE, 1929

Los Angeles, California, USA

RICHARD NEUTRA

Perched high up on a spur on the edge of the densely planted Griffith Park, the Lovell Health House has dramatic views over the Los Angeles suburbs. It is an early example of domestic steel construction, and this large, three-story, flat-roofed structure with extensive glazing has stood out from its neighbors since it was built. It was the first of Neutra's steel-frame houses, and the building's design employs contemporary ideas about rational planning and the importance of outdoor life. It is significant in terms of its structure—a steel frame prefabricated in sections and assembled on site, which was innovative at the time—and for its rapid construction process. Balconies are suspended from the roof frame by thin steel cables. Along the enclosing walls, the frame is subdivided into three, with steel casements for glazing.

FLATZ HOUSE, 2002

Schaan, Liechtenstein

BAUMSCHLAGER EBERLE

The Flatz House is for a country doctor and his large family, and is located on a sloping site facing the small town of Schaan, with a crest of mountains behind it. From outside, it is not immediately apparent that the house, a compact stack of rectilinear volumes made from maize yellow pigmented concrete, stretches over four levels, given its position on the slope. A staircase leads from the outside down into a double-height hall in the large, rectangular basement, which contains a cellar and a garage, and an independent apartment. An L-shaped ground floor houses the main kitchen and living rooms. The parents' floor above acts as a hinge, leading to the children's floor, a partly cantilevered horizontal slab. Green stone and plantain wood are used for unfussy detailing, maintaining the simplicity of the exterior.

MASCARA HOUSE, 2011

Shizuoka, Shizuoka Prefecture, Japan

MA-STYLE ARCHITECTS

The center of this H-shaped house is raised up off the ground and curves delightfully, like the hull of a boat. One wing of the home is used for sleeping and bathing, and the other for eating and playing; the central section forms a shared living area. Beyond and behind this are two terraces, the curves of both providing sheltered and comfortable nooks for lounging and enjoying good weather. The narrow wings are substantially enclosed: their high, unadorned walls anticipate possible future development on adjacent sites, and also protect the house to the east and west. The central living area has views over paddy fields and toward mountains. Wood is utilized inside, for cladding the walls and also for simple built-in furniture, which continues the nautical aesthetic—and addresses the client's taste for a natural-feeling building.

VILLA BUSK, 1990

Bamble, Norway

SVERRE FEHN

Situated on rocky terrain along the Oslofjorden, the Villa Busk is anchored to the sloping ground with solid concrete walls, which give way to a lighter, timber-constructed roof. Sometimes called the "poet of the straight line," Fehn plays on this theme in the rational plan of the house, built along the "internal route" of a single corridor that runs its entire length. The adjoining four-story tower, reached by a glazed bridge, has children's rooms on the lower level and a study above, connected by a spiral stair. Avoiding a sensationalist "signature" style, Fehn's thoughtful use of materials such as wood and concrete creates a tension with the natural surroundings by the undisguised human intervention. Fehn's work was cited by the Pritzker Prize jury for "a fascinating and exciting combination of modern forms tempered by the Scandinavian tradition."

FARNSWORTH HOUSE, 1951

Plano, Illinois, USA

LUDWIG MIES VAN DER ROHE

The view of the Farnsworth House through the trees is one of the greatest delights of Modernist architecture. The most exquisite of the glass-box houses, it hangs from a steel frame, its travertine floor suspended well above ground level, which is prone to heavy flooding from the nearby Fox River. It was designed as the perfect weekend retreat, a single volume completely open to view, with an elegant, timber-veneered service core enclosing a fireplace on one side, kitchen and services on the other and a bathroom at each end. Its open entrance porch occupies one-third of the entire floor space. As the ultimate example of International Style minimalism applied to domestic living, the house has been widely quoted and inspired Philip Johnson's later designed, but earlier completed Glass House (1949) in New Canaan, Connecticut.

ISLAND HOUSES, 2014

Gothenburg, Sweden

THAM & VIDEGÅRD ARKITEKTER

Elevated on a rocky outcrop on a Swedish west coast island, this low-rise retreat is surrounded by a skeletal wooden frame that gives it a templelike quality. Architects Tham & Videgård designed this project as a pair of identical homes for a family—one for the parents, one for their adult children—with room for guests. Each house is a simple square glass box perched on a podium constructed from local stone, set against the protruding bedrock, which has been recycled from ruined fishermen's cottages, and each has a spacious concrete terrace. The wooden structure defines the generous outdoor space and creates an austere loggia that neatly encloses each dwelling. Access stairs to the houses are cut into the solid base; apart from a few steps and stone walls, little has been added to the environment.

ECKER ABU ZAHRA HONEY HOUSE, 2006

Luftenberg, Austria

HERTL ARCHITEKTEN

Luftenberg is a small market town on the Danube, near Linz. The owners of this house, a teacher and sociologist, are also beekeepers running a business based on honey and beeswax products. Hertl designed them a simple cuboid volume, with a ground plan of 49 by 49 feet (15 by 15 meters). Rooms are in an L-shaped configuration on both stories; the heart of the home is a galleried double-height space on the ground floor with honey-colored walls for product presentations. The copper-clad facade features cutaways to open up views of the garden and landscape around the house. Next to the Honey House is a Corten steel–clad Bienothek, or apiary—the two adjacent buildings generate an avenue at the beginning of the site. Part of the garden serves as a specially planted meadow for the bees.

HAUS FREUDENBERG, 1908

Berlin, Germany

HERMANN MUTHESIUS

In his capacity as technical attaché to the Imperial German Embassy in London, between 1896 and 1903, Muthesius published work on the English country house and architects of the late nineteenth century. Webb, Shaw, Lutyens, Voysey, and others had developed a style of domestic building for a new middle class, adapted from the vernacular of the English countryside. Muthesius so admired this style that he sought to emulate it when he began his own firm on his return to Berlin. This house is one of the most obviously influenced by the English model. Its butterfly-shaped plan, embracing the entrance courtyard on one side and the garden to the rear, is taken directly from that of The Barn (1896) in Exmouth, Devon by E. S. Prior. However, the steep roofs, with their eyebrow dormers, reflect a middle European rather than an English vernacular.

CAPTAIN'S HOUSE, 2017

Fuzhou, Fujian, China

VECTOR ARCHITECTS

Captain's House overlooks the sea on the Huangqi Peninsula, in an area that features flat-roofed concrete apartment blocks and older stone cottages. The structure had originally been built for a sea captain some twenty years previously, and was suffering from water damage and decaying concrete, in part due to its flat roof collecting rain. Vector Architects were commissioned to restore the home, and added a vaulted roof, which gives the house a singular aesthetic. Windows are treated as "window-furniture systems" in the seam of the house, serving as separate space between external elements and the interior. Positioned beneath the curved roof is an open-plan floor of multifunctional space; here, glass bricks in the facade allow light inside. This space is used as a gym, activity room, and place of prayer.

RESIDENCIA OLGA, 1990

São Paulo, Brazil

MARCOS ACAYABA

A modern, inverted ziggurat forms the daring structure of this home. Built on a steeply sloping site, the project was conceived by Acayaba as a prototype of standardized housing for highly uneven hill sites common in Brazilian cities. Six concrete columns, sunk into the ground, provide the support for an industrialized wooden structure which is tied to the slope higher up for further stability. Three regular bays are divided into four levels of accommodation: the bottom three levels contain bedrooms, while the top level is an open-plan living, dining, and kitchen area. The house is entered from the top of the cliff at this level, and the grounds here are landscaped with a swimming pool and terrace. By using a modular system of bays, the cost and use of material is minimized, while the owners benefit from uninterrupted views.

HOUSE IN QUELFES, 2007
Olhão, Portugal

RICARDO BAK GORDON

Located in the eastern part of the Algarve, this one-story, three-bedroom house occupies a square plan. Four terraces—two at the north side of the house, two larger ones at the south—are cut away to create outdoor spaces. The roof pitches steeply in four directions from a leveled-off, central square. Where the roof ends, reed awnings continue, providing cover for the terraces; light shines through them to create beautifully abstract wall patterns. Inside, a sculptural roof creates a soaring, double-height space over the living areas and swoops down to make nestlike bedrooms with sloping ceilings. An airy and cool interior is a refuge from the outdoor terrace areas. Ricardo Bak Gordon gave the house a complex, stark geometry which is an arresting sight in the strong Algarve sun.

KAUFMANN DESERT HOUSE, 1947

Palm Springs, California, USA

RICHARD NEUTRA

Designed as a pavilion for inhabiting and encountering the arid desert of Palm Springs, the Kaufmann Desert House radiates out from its centre like a pinwheel, with each wing only one room wide in order to maximize the views of the surrounding scenery. The house sensitively adapts the International Style to this hot, harsh climate, using strong horizontal lines to contrast with the mountainous landscape. Neutra combines a Modernist vocabulary with a distinctive American accent, suggestive of Frank Lloyd Wright's Taliesin West. Here, however, the steel-frame house retains an intrusive presence, unlike Wright's organicism. This building fulfils Neutra's aspiration that his architecture combine "the goal of building environmental harmony, functional efficiency, and human enhancement into the experience of everyday living."

STRAND HOUSE, 2008

Rosslare, Ireland

O'DONNELL & TUOMEY

The Strand House, a vacation home by the beach, accommodates the distinct conditions of its site. An east-facing terrace provides views to the sea, and sheltered gardens are positioned to the west. Bedrooms, on the lower level, are protected from the road by a fuchsia hedge which has been planted within the structure of the retaining wall. As the house rises to the first floor, it reduces in volume, essentially forming a tower, to be in scale with neighboring houses. The architects chose to build the house predominantly from concrete, referencing the raw materials of the surrounding landscape, particularly the sand, seashells, and pebble stones of Rosslare Strand. O'Donnell & Tuomey first came to prominence with work on a much larger scale, including their regeneration of the run-down Temple Bar area of Dublin.

ITO HOUSE, 1998

Nagasaki, Nagasaki Prefecture, Japan

HIROSHI HARA

The Ito House consists of three discrete structures, with minimal openings, set in a forest in Nagasaki. Two exposed wood-shingle cubes are designated as wings for the parents and children, while a long corridor-like structure contains a study. Using cubes that progress in size in increments of 2 feet (0.6 meters), Hara examines whether there is a connection between arithmetical progression and behavioral patterns of the inhabitants of the cubes. He also suggests an alternative future society where the idea of community— in this case, of family—is dissolved and each individual, equipped with information technology, must devise his or her own world. This building composition not only expresses Hara's opinion on the pathological aspects of houses in contemporary society, but also his intensive exploration of an alternative typology.

MARIE SHORT HOUSE, 1975

Kempsey, New South Wales, Australia

GLENN MURCUTT

A long, low farmhouse on stilts, this single-family home owes much of its design to the woolsheds of New South Wales. With louvered walls, a curved roof to deflect rain, and an open-plan layout to keep air circulating, the Marie Short House fits with the architect's longstanding interest in developing an architecture that responds to landscape, climate, and local culture. The house consists of two overlapping rectangular volumes, open at opposite ends, divided into six bays connected by a corridor. Murcutt bought it for himself in 1980 and transformed the six bays into nine. The Pritzker Prize-winning architect works alone, and draws by hand. He is credited with putting Australian architecture on the map, and renowned for his fusion of vernacular and Modernist forms and materials: he was once described as "a timber and tin Miesian."

BJELLANDSBU CABIN, 2013

Etne, Norway

SNØHETTA

Sited in a rocky landscape layered with green grasses and heathers near Åkrafjorden, this mountain hut is only reachable on foot or by horseback. The basic structure is formed of two curved steel beams connected by a layer of hand-cut wooden planks. Its sloping roof is pitched at an angle similar to the nearby mountain peaks. The hut appears to grow out of the ground: it is made of local stone and tar-treated wood, with a traditional turf roof. The interior can accommodate twenty-one people snugly, with flexible seating for eating, socializing, and sleeping. The hut's graceful arching form suggests shelter and coziness. Viewed from afar, the cabin is almost entirely disguised amid the pools, crevices, and canyons of the surrounding landscape: only the stark concrete chimney indicates an island of human habitation.

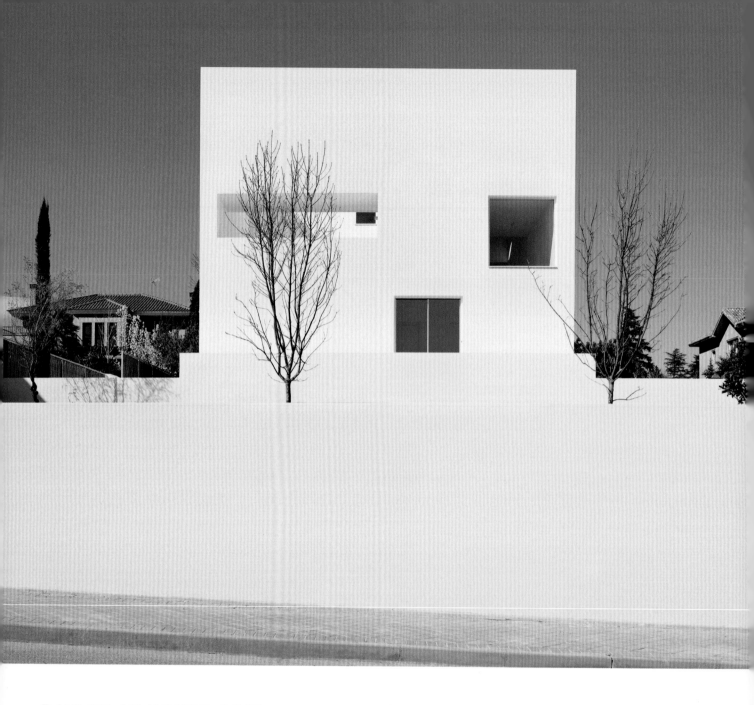

RAUMPLAN HOUSE, 2015
Madrid, Spain

ALBERTO CAMPO BAEZA

This home is a contemporary outworking of Adolf Loos's concept of Raumplan (spatial plan). The house is divided into four 20-by-20-foot (6-by-6-meter) spaces, stacked on top of each other, with a stairwell to the north. Single-height spaces stay on the same level, but double-height spaces are staggered by one story, allowing a diagonal visual connection between them. The facade is ornamentally blank, similarly to Loos's Villa Müller (1930), with windows, which appear to be placed randomly, corresponding to the planning of the interior, and it is colored a pristine white both inside and out. Numerous terraces, some spacious and others intimate, provide panoramic views over the Spanish capital. The Raumplan House is rendered serene by its clean lines, and a profound purity of space.

VILLA WAGNER II, 1913

Vienna, Austria

OTTO WAGNER

With its simple geometry, hierarchical rows of narrow windows, smooth walls, and restrained ornamentation, this house reflects Wagner's insistence on rationality as the basis for architectural beauty. A loggia on the right side overlooks a garden. Set off by a stepped frame, the front door is wood, but faced with a modern building material: aluminum. The decorative glazed tiles which underscore the design's geometric logic are held in place with aluminum bolts declaring their presence via large round heads. Wagner delighted in juxtaposing traditional materials with new ones, and expressiveness with economy of means. This house is considered among his purest Modernist statements. It contrasts with its next-door neighbor, the larger Villa Wagner I, a grand, ornate palais that proved too expensive for Wagner to maintain.

CRESCENT HOUSE, 2010

Encinitas, California, USA

WALLACE CUNNINGHAM

Although Cunningham is a graduate of the Chicago Academy of Fine Arts and the Frank Lloyd Wright School of Architecture, he is largely self-taught, which perhaps gives him more latitude to think outside the box with his designs. Located on the beachfront at Encinitas, this moon-inspired house has at its heart a beautiful crescent-shaped pool contained within a spiraling concrete ramp. Around this focal point, other orthogonal volumes are arranged. There is surprising geometry at every turn—a curve here, a sharp zigzag there. Cunningham is fascinated by the emotive qualities of light, using what he calls "lightscaping" on each project. Here, the house is a luminous space thanks to floor-to-ceiling glazing. "I'm interested in mystery and wonder," said Cunningham.

PITTMAN DOWELL RESIDENCE, 2009

Los Angeles, California, USA

MICHAEL MALTZAN

The clients for this house are Lari Pittman and Roy Dowell, who had formerly lived in the Richard Neutra–designed Serulnic House (1952) higher up the hillside. The two artists wanted to create another house that paid homage to Neutra, and they commissioned Maltzan for the project. The seven-sided white stucco building is a reinterpretation of Neutra's simple, orthogonal house—taking the angles of that, shifting them around, and transmuting them into something more complex and layered. Built around an irregularly shaped courtyard, the home is a series of interlocking polygons with a roof that pitches and folds multiple times like a piece of origami. The house provides expansive views over Los Angeles; inside, rooms are minimalistic and light-filled, with a shifting geometry that is joyful, enclosed, and dynamic.

SQUARE HOUSE, 2009

Karui-zawa, Nagano, Japan

MAKOTO TAKEI & CHIE NABESHIMA/TNA

This weekend house is sited on a narrow, sloping site, positioned on a ridge at the edge of a mountain. It has been designed to "float" in the woodland, upon seventy-six slender columns, some up to 26 feet (8 meters) high, which echo the form of the plentiful bamboo growing nearby in the forest. These square columns that support the building extend through the floor, as if the building foundation had grown from the ground, and penetrate the living spaces. Not all of them have a supporting function (many conceal water pipes and telecommunications wires)—some are decorative, and others delineate "rooms" defined by their minimal furnishings: daybed, dining table, kitchen counter, bathtub. An extensive use of glazing encircles the entire structure, and a large overhanging roof creates a slender canopy.

LEDGE HOUSE, 1996

Catoctin Mountains, Maryland, USA

BOHLIN CYWINSKI JACKSON

Built on a rocky and forested hillside in the Catoctin Mountains of Maryland, this house derives its name from the manmade ledge on which it has been constructed. The Ledge House replaces a traditional log cabin which had been built on this ridge in the 1940s, setting the precedent for the form of the building that was to follow. The architects used white cedar logs, heavy Douglas fir timbers, galvanized roofing metal, and a quartzite stone brought in from New York's Lake Champlain. This stone, while similar to the local stone, was chosen for its structural and aesthetic superiority. The features of the Ledge House include a massive fireplace constructed of the quartzite, a forecourt which provides an outdoor gathering space, and, surprisingly, an indoor pool. The logs and timbers are used to reinforce the concept that the house is an organic part of the forest.

MERRICKS HOUSE, 2009

Mornington Peninsula, Victoria, Australia

WOOD MARSH

The landscape around this house is lush, a patchwork of rolling vineyards. But on the Mornington Peninsula, the coastal climate can be harsh, prone to gale-force winds and sheeting rain. To address this, the Merricks House consists of a series of volumes which project from a central spine crafted of two crescent-shaped, rammed-earth walls. Rather than orientating the house for sea views, and the accompanying sea winds, the architects faced one side of its curve toward the hillside—this area is sheltered, and contains the outdoor living areas and a swimming pool; the other side has two blocks looking out to Western Port bay. As one walks through the central spine, openings punctuate the walls with brilliant vistas of the surrounding green fields. These variations in views dramatically vary the mood of different areas in the house.

HILL HOUSE, 1904

Helensburgh, Scotland, UK

CHARLES RENNIE MACKINTOSH

The Hill House is an extraordinary assembly of unusually detailed features. Windows of all shapes and sizes, stumpy chimneystacks, and round turrets—arbitrarily scattered about plain patches of walling and finished with traditional Scottish "harling" or rendering— give the house an ungainly lopsided appearance. Perhaps more greatly admired on the European continent than in his own country, Mackintosh had won second prize in a German competition for the design of "A House for a Connoisseur." For Hill House, he returned to a similarly asymmetrical design resulting from the novel layout of internal spaces building up into simple cubic volumes dominated by solid, unornamented shapes and a dash of Scottish baronial style. The architect is also celebrated for his exquisitely detailed, much reproduced furniture and stylized ornament.

SOFT-HARD ZINC HOUSE, 2014

Kokubunji, Tokyo, Japan

TERUNOBU FUJIMORI

Set on an average street in a town near Tokyo, the zinc cladding of this home has been tooled to create a padded effect, which is, according to the architect, "soft-hard." Appropriately, the building contains a textile museum and studio, and the residents jokingly refer to it as the "Chanel Handbag." The gabled end of the house cantilevers out dramatically, providing a parking space below. Minimal windows mean the interior feels snug and private. Fujimori is known for his eccentric dwellings, including his own house, which has dandelions growing from its facade. He built the Soft-Hard Zinc House with a group of volunteers called the Jomon Company, whose name references the Neolithic period of Japanese history—crafted using primitive tools, the interiors are finished with rough plaster and charred cedarwood.

ZACHARY HOUSE, 1999

Zachary, Louisiana, USA

STUDIO ATKINSON

This house in Zachary, Louisiana—the very first project built by Atkinson—is a variation on a humble housing type common throughout the southern USA, known as the "dogtrot": two rooms separated by an open breezeway. The house seems almost childlike in its simple profile, rustic corrugated metal exterior, and freestanding masonry chimney. However, the typical metal roof of Atkinson's dogtrot is exaggerated by a forty-five-degree pitch and corrugated metal siding (recalling the exteriors of nearby farm structures), the architect's own embellishments. Corrugated shutters at the ends of the house conceal glazed double doors. A long deck extends at a right angle from the house. This home, built for the architect's parents in the region where he grew up, shows how powerful even the most modest buildings can be.

HOUSE IN LUMINO, 2009

Lumino, Switzerland

DAVIDE MACULLO ARCHITETTO

This house echoes the traditional architecture of the centuries-old stone farmhouses in the village of Lumino, close to Bellinzona in the Swiss Alps, which are marked by their use of a single construction material. The house is designed as a geometric composition. With a cool, reinforced-concrete facade, the structure is in stark contrast to its verdant surroundings. The house is cut in the middle to create a dynamic connection to both exterior and interior. The interior contains a multifloor space defined by half-levels of two shifted parallelepipeds. Two bedrooms, both connecting to an outdoor terrace, are situated a half level up from the ground floor. The master bedroom at the next level has access to the garden below. The kitchen and dining areas open on to the main loggia, while principal living space is situated at the top.

LOUVER HOUSE, 2007

Wainscott, New York, USA

LEROY STREET STUDIO

Wainscott is a seaside town on the south shore of Long Island. The Louver House is situated next to vast corn and potato fields, and its design is inspired by the rural location. The barnlike house is utilitarian in form, and uses modest materials—predominantly teak—to blend in with the landscape. Continuous louvered screens wrap and unify the building to provide privacy and reduce its heavy massing. At night, light glows from within the house with a muted, gauzy quality. Inside, the double-height foyer is lofty and bright; an open-plan living, cooking, and dining area has a vaulted roof supported by teak and steel trusses, and a mezzanine study connects to a garden on the roof. The house is both somber and earthy in its aesthetic: a sensitive contemporary addition to the pastoral landscape.

BAROSSA HOUSE, 2012

Lyndoch, South Australia, Australia

MAX PRITCHARD ARCHITECT

This house crouches low into a hillside, drinking in views over the rolling landscape of the Barossa Valley. The building pursues the undulating slopes of the land with five level changes along its length, while the dynamic, bladelike roof rises diagonally; a continuous timber ramp links the different levels. The skinny, elongated plan means that all of the rooms face north, allowing the winter sun to warm the home naturally. Overhanging eaves provide generous shade in the summer, while the residence is naturally protected by berming on the eastern and southern walls, which provides thermal mass on cold winter days. The acidic yellow used on the roof is a cheery color, and makes a fantastic contrast with the green pastures surrounding the house and the bright cerulean skies above.

FLINT HOUSE, 2015
Waddesdon, England, UK

SKENE CATLING DE LA PEÑA

Constructed for Baron Jacob Rothschild within the grounds of Waddesdon Manor, the Flint House was initially intended as a domicile for the curator of the Rothschild archive. Now, however, the Rothschild family use it. The residence is clad with the flint that occurs naturally in the local Buckinghamshire fields. Arranged in graduating tones, the flint varies from a smoky gray at the bottom of the facade to paler chunks above, topped by blocks of white chalk: the entire thing represents both a geological and visual evolution. Its wedge-shaped form—a striking presence in the green English landscape—was Charlotte Skene Catling's response to the ploughed fields. "The site was a strange, still place," the architect has said. The residence won the RIBA House of the Year award in 2015.

VICTOR HORTA HOUSE, 1901

Brussels, Belgium

VICTOR HORTA

Victor Horta's private house with an adjacent studio at 23–5 rue Américaine was built between 1898 and 1901. The luscious Art Nouveau staircase inside demonstrates all the characteristics of the new style that had swept Europe in the late nineteenth century: whiplash lines, abstracted botanical and zoological decorative forms, asymmetry, a rich palette of color and materials—themes which unified the whole design. The exterior is characterized by its metal work, used for both structure and ornament. Horta had already designed many other buildings in this manner, notably the Hôtel Tassel (1893), Hôtel Solvay (1894), and Hôtel van Eetvelde (1895). The Art Nouveau style was comparatively short-lived, but it represents a major contribution to the extremely abundant creativity across Europe just before the birth of Modernism.

LOBLOLLY HOUSE, 2006

Taylors Island, Maryland, USA

KIERANTIMBERLAKE

Set amid a dense grove of loblolly pines, with views of Chesapeake Bay, this Taylors Island home minimizes its environmental impact by being raised off the ground on stilts, as well as through clever use of prefabrication. Instead of having thousands of individual components, the main parts of the house were simplified as much as possible into prebuilt elements. Modules—including entire bathrooms—were lowered into an aluminum frame "scaffold," as were cartridges containing either service equipment or insulation. All assembly could be done using simple hand tools. A red cedar rain screen re-creates the pattern of solids and voids of the forest wall. Through this, an orange-glass footbridge connects the two volumes of the Loblolly House; and as sunlight passes through the bridge, it glows.

PARATY HOUSE, 2009

Paraty, Brazil

STUDIO MK27

This luxurious, minimalist home is on an island off the coast of Paraty, with views of the ocean and lush rainforest. It consists of two long, stacked orthogonal boxes that are dug into a mountainside, the lower extending outward—almost onto the beach—with a 26 foot (8 meter) cantilever. Arriving by boat, visitors step onto the beach, then traverse a fantastical crystal-lined pool by bridge to enter the house via a stairway. The living, cooking, and dining spaces are on the lower floor, which spans 88½ feet (27 meters). The bedrooms are on the upper floor, and shaded by retractable eucalyptus screens. Bedrooms which face the mountainside have small internal patios and are additionally lit by skylights. An extensive use of board-formed concrete both inside and outside gives the Paraty House a brutalist aesthetic.

TWIN HOUSES, 2011

Kastanienbaum, Switzerland

LUSSI + HALTER

To make building their dream home more affordable, architect Remo Halter and his wife invited another couple, an artist and a doctor, to collaborate with them on two adjoining three-story dwellings near Lucerne, right on the shore of the lake. This brooding, black concrete mass is the result, hovering amid the woodland; openings in the facades offer selected views into the forest. The structure recalls Le Corbusier's Villa Savoye: a cantilevering first floor, ribbon windows, double carport, and ramp to sweep inhabitants to the upper levels (matching the angle of the ramp to the roof terrace at Savoye exactly). A shared roof terrace features a swimming pool. The house strikes a visual contrast with the surrounding nature, but this is part of its appeal. Halter has said: "The black box is powerful. You feel a certain energy emanating from it."

MYLLA HYTTE, 2017

Jevnaker, Norway

MORK ULNES ARCHITECTS

Hidden in a pine forest outside Oslo, this is Norwegian-born, U.S.-based architect Caspar Mork-Ulnes's contemporary take on the cabin in the woods. Planning regulations stipulated a gabled roof, but this design splits the gable in half and creates four shed roofs which radiate out in a pinwheel formation. Two sheltered outdoor spaces are created on either side of the cabin. The exterior is clad in untreated pine which will weather and become silver over time, eventually blending in with a snowy landscape. The interior is lined with simple plywood, which has also been used for custom-made beds, benches, a dining table, and shelving. A compact 940 square feet (87.3 square meters), snugly accommodating three bedrooms and two bathrooms, the home is perfectly suited for a family's weekend getaways.

HOUSE AT CAMUSDARACH SANDS, 2013

Highlands, Scotland, UK

RAW ARCHITECTURE WORKSHOP

Situated on a steeply raked Scottish Highlands hillside, on land formerly used as rough grazing pasture for livestock, House at Camusdarach Sands was built for a young local couple. They wanted a home whose orientation would maximize views of the sun as it rises over the mountains to the east and sets behind the islands to the west. The home has a distinctive double-gabled form—referencing the traditional gabled farmhouses nearby—which features large banks of windows at either end to facilitate views. The roof dips toward the foundation forming a saddle between the gables; the middle volume mitigates the structural exposure to the harsh elements. The upper portion of the home is clad in vertical timber planks, which have been stained black in a nod to the abundant peat and gorse growing nearby.

GARCIA HOUSE, 1962

Los Angeles, California, USA

JOHN LAUTNER

Hovering above Mulholland Drive on V-shaped stilts, an eye-shaped house gazes down over the canyon below. Named after its owner Russell Garcia, a jazz composer, it was nicknamed "the Rainbow House" for its stained-glass windows and arching shape. With a void bisecting the two halves of the house, an outside spiral staircase connects both parts, forcing occupants to regularly go outside—and soundproofing Garcia's music work from other inhabitants. In 2002 it received an extensive renovation by a local practice, expert in midcentury Modern architecture, Marmol Radziner. A towering figure of twentieth-century American architecture, Lautner said that when planning a building, he sought "its particular and unique expression with all the senses." Without a doubt, this can be seen with the Garcia House.

CRESCENT HOUSE, 2008

Minami-Hakone, Shizuoka, Japan

SHIGERU BAN

This arcing, C-shaped house in a hot-spring resort was designed to provide panoramic views of Mount Fuji. Its inwardly tapering shape also gives privacy from neighboring residences. Built into the side of a slope in the Atami mountain range and elevated on steel poles, the house has a steel-frame construction, and a glass-wrapped staircase at ground level gives access to the first floor. Bedrooms are at either end of the crescent where it narrows to points, with living spaces in between them at the deepest section. Inside, the floors, walls, and ceiling are clad in a pale Japanese cypress wood. The organic, shell-like space creates a feeling of warm enclosure on the one hand but, on the other, feels totally open to nature. The structure is now rented out as a location for filming and photo shoots.

EAMES HOUSE, 1949

Pacific Palisades, California, USA

CHARLES & RAY EAMES

Lightweight, steel-and-glass, and in the perpetual sunshine of southern California, the Eames house, also known as Case Study House No. 8, presented an enticing image to other architects, but especially to British architects: Norman Foster, Richard Rogers, John Winter, and Michael Hopkins have all paid tribute to it. If one building launched British High-Tech, this is it. The modern house and its associated studio behind create as much space as possible using minimal materials. Developing an identifiable aesthetic out of such practical construction gave it an enduring place in the canon of great architectural works. Elevating the ordinary, the everyday, and "found objects" became the husband-and-wife team's hallmark, particularly in the eclectic mix of artfully ordered objects inside the house.

RURAL ICELANDIC COTTAGES, 2015

Brekkuskógur, Iceland

PKDM ARKITAKTUR

The lakeside area of Brekkuskógur, in southwest Iceland, is a landscape of open vistas. Here, a collection of wooden cottages has been nested in the fields to create a semirural residential enclave; these are the two prototypes designed by PKdM. Powered by geothermal energy from specially drilled sources on the site, they have close to zero carbon footprint. Clad in charred hardwood batons, the houses peek just above the grass line and create dark silhouettes in the landscape. The turf roofs, which reference Icelandic vernacular architecture, recycle vegetation from the site excavation. Earth dug from the plot was also used to build the wind-protecting bunker enclosing the outdoor terraces, and to fuse the grass roof with the surrounding slope. These houses, through simple techniques, gently contrast with the landscape.

CASA EN EL CAMPO, 2007

Artà, Spain

JUAN HERREROS ARQUITECTOS

In northeastern Mallorca, an existing vernacular structure, which formerly served as a refuge for shepherds, was used as the starting point for an expanded rural home. The sawtooth-shaped roof came as a result of symmetrically duplicating the original building's form to create two different facades. The house's flank walls are kept in local stone, while the front and rear facades are clad in pale green corrugated metal. Shutters hinge back across the windows to reveal a smooth underside, creating a rhythm of polished and rippling surfaces. The interior reproduces the original, primitive scheme of three compartments (for animals, shepherds, and forage) and splits it facing two directions: north (kitchen, bedroom, and bathroom) and south (dining room, living room, and study), creating a sensitive space for pleasure, rest, and contemplation of the landscape.

PALAIS STOCLET, 1911

Brussels, Belgium

JOSEF HOFFMANN

The flat, white marble walls, elaborate bronze trimmings and part-romantic, part-industrial-style staircase tower of this house mark a watershed in architectural styles. It is both the most important home of the Secession movement and the crossover point between nineteenth-century and Modernist architecture. The fifty-roomed mansion, designed for the Belgian industrialist Adolphe Stoclet, is a massive, total work of art, or *Gesamtkunstwerk*, where all furniture and furnishings are integrated into the design concept. Twinned Gustav Klimt mirror-image murals are features of the dining room. The building is comparatively free in its plan, dominated by the paradoxically plain tower, elaborately adorned with statues. Both old-style palace and new-age industrial machine for living, the Palais Stoclet is one in a long line of great European townhouses.

SKYWOOD HOUSE, 1999

Middlesex, England, UK

GRAHAM PHILLIPS

Skywood House, located in Denham, Middlesex, is the very image of a pure, minimalist home that might be straight out of Hollywood. Set in a large wooded walled garden, between a black swimming pool and an artificial lake, the house is an exploration of geometric space, glass, and reflected surfaces; indeed, water is a principal element here, in the tradition of Japanese gardens. The Skywood House is precisely constructed, and has a polished limestone floor which extends from the interior space to exterior. Beneath the canopies of brise-soleil, light and shade are bisected to create rigorous, orthogonal lines. Transparency is treated as a craft rather than a byproduct. Skywood fulfills the architect's aspiration for a "glass box in the woods"—dematerializing the relationship between outside and inside.

HIROSHIMA HUT, 2014

Hiroshima, Hiroshima Prefecture, Japan

SUPPOSE DESIGN OFFICE

The Hiroshima Hut is designed to get the inhabitants as close as possible to nature—and nature as close as possible to them. The architects designed it as part observation spot, part living space. A lightweight overhanging roof creates a shelter to entice local wildlife, such as the deer that regularly emerge from nearby woods. The span of the roof's overhang equals the height of the house, and it sits on walls of acrylic, chosen over glass for better insulation. There are no supporting beams in the structure; it's possible to see through one side of it to the other. Within the open-plan interior, different zones are enclosed by metal mesh to allow further visual permeability through the house. The kitchen and bathroom are within square sunken spaces in the floor, providing some privacy from curious animals.

IWATA HOUSE, 1963

Monterey Park, California, USA

PIERRE KOENIG

Built for Richard and Viki Iwata and their five children, 912 Summit Place is in an elevated position with stunning views over Los Angeles. The three-story house, with floors stacked in an inverted ziggurat, connects to a one-story outdoor barbecue pavilion via two bridges spanning a leafy courtyard area. The site also contains a pool at the front. This project features more extensive glazing than any other in Koenig's oeuvre. To keep the nearly all-glass house cool, concrete fins creating a brise-soleil were installed on street- and valley-facing elevations, giving the house a distinctly brutalist aesthetic—unusual for 1960s Modernist villas. This feature was also a radical shift for Koenig, who generally designed simpler, steel-framed structures, such as the celebrated Stahl House (1959), which was built as part of the Case Study House Program.

HOUSE 20, 2010

Toorak, Victoria, Australia

JOLSON ARCHITECTURE

This three-story house in the Melbourne suburb of Toorak makes imaginative use of the sculptural qualities of concrete. The front of the house features eight astonishing cantilevered blades that appear to rest on a bronze garden wall. It is built on a slope, and visitors enter via the middle floor. The ground-floor living space is divided by a glass atrium, and intense daylight entering it is softened by wire mesh. The house features a roof terrace, library, home office, and master suite. The interior space is designed to integrate indoor and alfresco zones and can be configured in a variety of ways—for example, the study at the front of the house can be portioned off to form a bedroom. For leisure and relaxation, there is a lap pool, steam room, and gym. The honed Australian bluestone walkways contrast with American oak flooring.

HOPKINS HOUSE, 1976

London, England, UK

MICHAEL & PATTI HOPKINS

In 1976 Michael Hopkins, after working with Norman Foster, set up his own practice with his wife, Patty. Choosing a plot on Downshire Hill, a road of handsome Regency villas in Hampstead, London, the couple designed an experimental family home and studio. Relatively inexpensive to build, the house used prefabricated elements, and had an open and flexible interior, and exposed steel structures—features associated with the High-Tech movement in architecture, which critic Reyner Banham hailed as "alternative Modernism." From the street, the two-story residence appears as one story, as the plot is sunk below the road. The entrance is reached via a drawbridge, giving Hopkins House a sense of apartness. Front and back facades are utterly transparent, and the house radiates a pragmatic and calm efficiency.

MAGNEY HOUSE, 1984

Bingie Point, New South Wales, Australia

GLENN MURCUTT

Glenn Murcutt's Magney House is situated between the ocean and bush land in splendid isolation on the remote south coast of New South Wales. Envisioned as a response to the climate and site, the house is located below a ridge line, facing north to the sea. The building is divided by a courtyard that forms two self-contained suites. Its northern face has glazed sliding screens and external louvers, regulating temperature, and the cantilevered roof provides shade from the summer sun and also collects rainwater that is recycled for drinking and heating. The tubular steel frame, which is an extremely light skeleton, is a continuation of Murcutt's earlier work. Features now taken for granted as sustainable elements found early expression and form in this structure. This is an understated house that is sensitive to its rural environment.

MIMETIC HOUSE, 2007

Dromahair, Ireland

DOMINIC STEVENS ARCHITECTS

Mimetic House, positioned in the center of a green, hilly landscape, is prismatic in form, with angled mirrored facades. The building is at once an element in contrast with its surroundings and—due to its reflective characteristics—able, in certain light, to almost become camouflaged against it: a true act of mimesis. The lower level of the dwelling, where the entrance and the sleeping and study quarters are located, is semiconcealed below ground. The main living space above is bright and light, with a rhythm of uniformly positioned windows. The dramatic angular shape of the exterior is experienced on the inside, where the eye is drawn up and outward. At the room's center are the components required for comfortable contemplation of the landscape: a wood-burning stove, a simple space for food preparation, and a convivial seating arrangement.

CASA ORGÁNICA, 1984

Naucalpan, Mexico

JAVIER SENOSIAIN

Born in 1948, Senosiain is a key figure in the organic architecture movement. This house in Naucalpan, northwest of Mexico City, is built partly in the shape of a shark. An undulating ferroconcrete construction with bulbous projections is partially buried under turf, merging with nature. The creature's wide open jaws provide a panoramic window to the valley below. The house's polyurethane skin is reptilian, glimmering with iridescent colors. Eyelike windows are placed irregularly. Inside, it is a softly curving, dark, enclosed space with built-in furniture and shelving. According to Senosiain, such organic architecture brings humans closer to their original selves. "The concept of an organic habitat," he has written, "is the creation of spaces adapted to man which are also similar to a mother's bosom or an animal's lair."

MAISON DE VERRE, 1932

Paris, France

PIERRE CHAREAU

The translucence of the Maison de Verre's glass blocks, and the precision of its black steel framing and red oxide accents, are reminiscent of an inlaid black-lacquered Japanese box. This three-story house, built as a doctor's residence with a surgery at ground floor level, is inserted into the void of an eighteenth-century courtyard, and is one of the canonical works of the twentieth century. Light filters into the open-plan interior via the two glass facades, and the framing device of the exterior steel ladder is continued inside in the slender, vertical forms that punctuate the floor plan. Collaborating with Dutch architect Bernard Bijvoet, Chareau created a house with a sensual urbanity, unique for its inventive handling of ready-made materials, its deployment of suspended and sliding components, and a refinement of details.

CASA O'GORMAN, 1929

Mexico City, Mexico

JUAN O'GORMAN

The muralist and architect Juan O'Gorman designed this residence on two tennis courts when he was just twenty-four: it is his own outworking of a Corbusian *machine à habiter*. Widely considered Latin America's first functionalist house, it strikes a sublime balance between angular forms and curves—its boxlike, cantilevering upper level counterpointing the swooping helicoidal concrete staircase. The red-earth color and cactus fence are vernacular details typical of the Mexican postrevolutionary period. It impressed Diego Rivera, who commissioned O'Gorman to build two connecting studios for himself and Frida Kahlo. Later in his career, O'Gorman abandoned formalism, declaring it to be "mechanically reasonable and humanly illogical because man is not a machine," and firmly turned toward a more organic architecture.

BUTLER HOUSE, 1937
Des Moines, Iowa, USA

EARL BUTLER & GEORGE KRAETSCH

Described by an American magazine in 1937 as "the world's most modern house," this house was commissioned by engineer Earl Butler, who wanted a space for entertaining. The twenty-eight-room home was a superb example of the Streamline Moderne style of the 1930s, a later version of Art Deco. Built of reinforced concrete, with metal-framed windows, it excelled in its use of technology, featuring air-conditioning, garbage disposal, electric garage doors, an intercom system, and dishwashers. In the dining room, lighting could be adjusted to accent the attire of guests. A Corbusian ramp was used for internal circulation, rather than a staircase, and there was a secret passageway to the wine cellar. Following remodeling work by ASK Studio, the Butler House has been adapted for use as offices and has had a courtyard and auditorium added.

MASTERS' HOUSES, 1926

Dessau, Germany

WALTER GROPIUS

Founded by Walter Gropius in 1919, the Bauhaus school of design in Dessau was one the world's most important crucibles of avant-garde Modernism; its zenith years were between 1925 and 1932. Gropius designed three pairs of semidetached houses for the school's "masters" (teachers who took a lead in different subject areas) and a detached house for the Bauhaus director. Residents included a coterie of celebrity Modernists, such as László Moholy-Nagy, Wassily Kandinsky, Paul Klee, and Mies van der Rohe. The houses, following functionalist design principles, are planned in roughly S-shaped interlocking cuboid forms, with generous glazing facing the street to illuminate the built-in studios. Colored accents were added to the undersides of balconies, window reveals, and drainpipes. The complex was renovated in 1992.

RICHARD H. MANDEL HOUSE, 1935

Bedford Hills, New York, USA

EDWARD DURELL STONE

This house represents Stone's first major independent project: a commission from retailer Richard H. Mandel to build a home in Westchester County, an hour north of Manhattan. Previously, Stone had designed New York's Art Deco Radio City Music Hall (1932) as part of the team working on the Rockefeller Center. The Z-shaped house was met with great acclaim: wholeheartedly embracing the International Style, it showed influences from Le Corbusier and Erich Mendelsohn. The steel-framed, concrete-block and white stucco mansion achieved a bold, almost brutal horizontality, with expansive ribbon windows, a curving tower, and projecting balconies sat on piloti. Stone would go on to design the Museum of Modern Art in New York, before falling out of favor with the architectural community because of his opulent American embassy (1959) in New Delhi.

WALDEN HOUSE, 2009

Edwards, Colorado, USA

SELLDORF ARCHITECTS

Situated west of Vail, Colorado, within the White River National Forest mountain range at an elevation of 8,200 feet (2,500 meters), Walden House's main living spaces are orientated toward a new pond and take advantage of the spectacular views of the surrounding Gore Range and New York Mountains. The seven-bedroom complex consists of a series of smaller volumes arranged around a central quadrangle, the enclosure creating an intimate counterpoint to the grandeur and scale of the surrounding mountain landscape. The interpretation of indoor and outdoor spaces fuses the architecture with its natural setting. Local materials, including copper, field rock, log-pole siding, and stacked beetle-kill pine wood, reinforce the relationship between the buildings and their high mountain environment.

TRANSUSTAINABLE HOUSE, 2014

Chofu, Tokyo, Japan

SUGAWARADAISUKE

This house, built on a typically small plot in Tokyo, playfully obscures the boundaries between inside and outside. With an area of 409 square feet (38 square meters), the house contains private spaces which are placed on diagonals at opposite corners—on the ground floor, a bedroom and multipurpose room, the second floor, a kitchen and bedroom—with common space either side of them, in cut-out voids which create inner courtyards. These semi-indoor areas have pebbled floors and extensive windows to maximize the connection with outdoor space and increase the home's natural ventilation. The distinctive rusted facade, a mix of powdered iron and plaster, gives it an industrial look and shows the traces of the microclimate over time. Its simple form appears to mimic that of the archetypal child's drawing of a house.

SHIROKANE HOUSE, 2013

Minato, Tokyo, Japan

MDS

The concrete facade of this family home in Tokyo was shaped by a challenging brief: to create a comfortable house on a small site that maximizes space. Silent and faceted, this chamfered volume is configured to ameliorate all these requirements, as well as eking out maximum daylight. Its bulging skin pushes upward and outward, giving greater volume to the upper-level living spaces. The sole aperture in the shutter-marked facade is the front door. While the exterior appears dark and lithic, this contrasts with interiors which are "carved" out of the concrete volume. A central void spans between roof and kitchen level, and interconnecting staircases are crafted from delicate black steel. Exposed concrete finishes that reveal the shutter-marked in situ construction are simply left raw, complemented by walls painted white.

ROOS HOUSE, 1909

San Francisco Bay area, California, USA

BERNARD MAYBECK

Designed by the architect of the Palace of Fine Arts in San Francisco, the Roos House takes on a more medieval character. A facade of ornamental, half-timber framework of redwood, infilled with stucco, supports quatrefoil tracery, reflecting Maybeck's early experience in furniture design and adding a sense of whimsy to the house. That which appears ornamental on the exterior becomes structural on the interior, with the heavy redwood beams demonstrably supporting the double-story living room in the manner of an Art and Crafts manor house. The house has an innovative raftlike foundation, which permits the structure to rock during earthquakes and eliminates the need for heavy foundation walls. The overall composition of the Roos House set the tone for the informal fantasy of the Bay area styles to come.

KIRSCH RESIDENCE, 1982

Oak Park, Illinois, USA

ERROL J. KIRSCH

In a suburb predominantly full of heritage architecture, including Frank Lloyd Wright's home and studio, the Kirsch residence is a surprising anomaly. Massive in scale, it is built in an irregular ziggurat form with spiky, sharply pitched roofs. Its facade is a series of projections and recessions broken up by a grille of slit windows with brise-soleils—giving it an unmistakable resemblance to Darth Vader's helmet. The architect's key priority was energy efficiency: the concrete enclosure effectively inhibits temperature variation, and windows are designed to maximize solar gain. The tall chimney may be part of a heat stack strategy. There is a strong sense of enclosure and security that does not merely come from the heavy materiality of the concrete, but also from the geometric forms Kirsch chose.

18.36.54, 2010

South Kent, Connecticut, USA

DANIEL LIBESKIND

This chocolate-colored structure is designed as one folded plan, sited in a meadow in the Connecticut countryside. The client wanted a mixture of the avant-garde and the cozy, so Libeskind clad the home in mirror-finish, bronzed stainless steel. The house selectively incorporates the elements: it doesn't blend in; rather, the lustrous cladding accentuates the changes of light and season to create a sensuous object. The house's name derives from the number of the planes (eighteen), points (thirty-six), and lines (fifty-four) that the spiraling ribbon facade makes as it defines the living space of the dwelling. Interior finishes and built-in furniture are custom-made from locally harvested white oak, and porches on every side provide unimpeded views of the surrounding fields. This house is thrilling, mysterious, and beyond language.

SUN VALLEY HOUSE, 2013

Sun Valley, Idaho, USA

RICK JOY ARCHITECTS

The knife-sharp geometry of this Idaho stone house is inspired by, and a counterpoint to, the softer shapes of the surrounding mountains. The upper parts of the retreat have been wrapped in a sleek skin of interlocking steel panels whose lightness and reflectivity emphasize the angular forms. On a west-facing plot, the house was carefully positioned on a steep hillside to maximize views, and the Y-shaped plan splits it into two wings; the wooden ceiling rafters inside draw the eye down and out to the extensive terrain. The western wing, which is two stories, is partly embedded in the mountainside to minimize visual impact, while the eastern one is a single level. The volumes huddle together in the landscape, creating an enclosed, welcoming entrance courtyard. Care was taken to preserve the abundant native sage growing on the site.

SEIDLER HOUSE, 1967

Killara, New South Wales, Australia

HARRY SEIDLER &
PENELOPE SEIDLER

A steep site bounded by a creek and a nature reserve was exactly the secluded, leafy location that Penelope and Harry Seidler had been seeking for their own house. Located in Sydney's Killara neighborhood, the split-level plan gives a comfortable family home attuned to the landscape and Sydney's climate. The house's four half-levels are organized about a central open atrium that links all floors; access is from the top of the plot via a suspended concrete bridge. At the time, the textural reinforced concrete composed in horizontal and vertical planes was revolutionary; most suburban Australian homes cleaved to bungalows of lapped timber or brick and tile. Instead, the Seidler House engages with its natural setting through open volumes, heightened by stone walls and ceilings of Tasmanian oak.

HOUSE IN YATSUGATAKE, 2012

Chino, Nagano, Japan

KIDOSAKI ARCHITECTS STUDIO

"It is almost as if you are living on a cloud," architect Hirotaka Kidosaki has said of this dramatically cantilevering house in Chino. He explained his two priorities: to blend into the natural surroundings and to maximize views as far as possible. A long, narrow structure, its form is a flattened abstraction of the low mountains it faces on the horizon. The one-story, three-bedroom home rests on a steel-framed, reinforced-concrete pedestal dug into the hillside, with the cantilevering platform further supported by two diagonal steel cylinders. Sliding back the floor-to-ceiling glazing lets in the mountain breeze. The art of cloud gazing was an ancient Japanese way of predicting the future; the expansive decked terrace here is the perfect spot to relax, contemplate, and dream.

CASA CANDELARIA, 2016

San Miguel de Allende, Mexico

CHEREM ARQUITECTOS

In a grove of prickly pears, this home is built in the style of the Mexican hacienda, with twelve main volumes organized around two courtyards, which are shaded by a concrete roof. It is located on the outskirts of the city of San Miguel de Allende. The walls of the single-story house resemble concrete but are actually made with rammed earth, excavated from the site. This kept costs down and helps the home stay cool. Natural pigments were added to create the gray finish. Casa Candelaria has a stark yet sleek simplicity that is utterly in harmony with its arid environment. The living spaces are defined by open circulation; two interior corridors connect the private areas of the house with patios, terraces, a swimming pool, and gardens. This internal arrangement allows for the surrounding valley to be pulled into focus from any room.

CELANESE HOUSE, 1959
New Canaan, Connecticut, USA

EDWARD DURELL STONE

Edward Durell Stone was at the height of his fame when he was commissioned to design this house in the comfortable suburb of New Canaan. It was intended as a showcase for the Celanese Corporation, a chemical manufacturer specializing in plastics and fibers. Stone had already designed the Museum of Modern Art in New York two decades previously with Philip L. Goodwin, and it's a testament to his high repute that the corporation would only consider Stone or Frank Lloyd Wright for the commission. The one-story house, distinctive for the twelve pyramidal skylights, is largely hidden behind by a delicate screen of crisscrossing white wooden slats. The design demonstrates Stone's fascination with classical motifs. It received national attention when it was completed, and was later sold as a private dwelling.

BOOK HOUSE, 2005

Shikine-jima, Tokyo, Japan

NENDO

Tucked in between a hedge and a hillside on an island south of Tokyo, this unusual house by nendo is part private dwelling, part public library. Bookshelves clad the exterior walls; an overhanging roof creates a verandalike space, making two sides of the house open. This encourages visitors to wander in, and browse and borrow from the collection of reading materials. The internal walls of the home are made of a semitranslucent fiber-reinforced plastic. When viewed from the inner living space, the arrangement of books on the shelves creates a lattice pattern of ghostly beauty. At night, light seeps through the whole structure, and, viewed from the exterior, it appears to radiate warmth and life. For security and privacy, the house can be enclosed by wooden shutters, which wrap around the whole veranda.

MAISON À BORDEAUX, 1998

Gironde, France

OMA

The striking structure of this house was intended to give it a feeling of "launch." The concrete box forming the upper floor, containing the bedrooms, appears to float across the glazed middle level on which the main living space is situated. The equilibrium of the house is maintained by a steel beam overhead, anchored to the ground by a cable. The dramatized approach to the building structure suggests a flouting of the laws of rational expression enshrined in the Modernist functionalist tradition. At the same time, the system of delicate balances creates a dynamic domestic landscape which, with an open elevator room at its heart, meets the wheelchair-user client's desire for a house which "will define my world." As such, it is very much a part of the OMA tradition of designing urban and suburban landscapes around intricate organizational narratives.

HOUSE, DORDOGNE, 1997
Dordogne, France

LACATON & VASSAL

Close to a river bordered with poplar trees, in a quintessentially French rural landscape is this unusual, long, low-lying house. It has an archetypal barnlike form. The house is split into distinct parts—one for living, cooking, and studying, the other for sleeping. Between the two areas is a large conservatory-like space with a transparent roof, given ample ventilation through roof openings and glazing that slides open. The east, west, and south elevations feature a regular rhythm of openings that give framed views of the countryside. But when required, these can be closed off with shutters, making the house resemble an introverted, sealed box; the shimmering effect of the sun's rays reflecting off the metallic cladding gives an almost magical presence to the otherwise simple structure.

BRYANT HAYBALE HOUSE, 1995

Hale County, Alabama, USA

RURAL STUDIO

Protected by the embrace of a large front porch, inhabitants can watch the night fall from this house in rural Alabama. The family—at the time of construction, two grandparents and their three young grandchildren—used to live in a shack without plumbing or heating before this house was designed and built for them, free of charge, by a group of students from Auburn University. It was the first project for Rural Studio, an educational and sociological initiative, which brings students to impoverished Hale County as an element of their architectural training. They are responsible for every step of the process, from meeting with the client to completing the design and working as the construction crew. In an effort to reduce costs, the walls of this house are made of hay bales rendered in stucco, and the floor is a concrete slab covered with bricks.

301

CREEK VEAN, 1966

Cornwall, England, UK

TEAM 4

Constructed from humble materials—predominantly concrete blocks that are worked to an extraordinary level of precision—Creek Vean is a response to the steep and uneven landscape. The central steps are a major organizational element; they both separate and unite the two sleeping and living wings, while connecting different levels and providing an external space from which to enjoy the view. Team 4 comprised Richard Rogers, Norman Foster, Wendy Cheesman, and Su Brumwell. It is said that the difficulty they had in achieving their required level of detail with the wet trades (concrete, plaster, and mortar) used here put them off working with traditional techniques. All the later work of Rogers and Foster uses industrial prefabricated elements, a predominant feature of the High-Tech architecture that emerged in the 1970s.

HOUSE FOR A DRUMMER, 2016

Karna, Sweden

BORNSTEIN LYCKEFORS

This house was built for a single father whose interests included drumming, sailing, and nature. He wanted a countryside home for weekends with his two children that could be a social space, but also intimate when he was alone. Built predominantly of wood, the house is painted Swedish *falu* red. An open section cut through the house allows light to permeate all spaces. The ground floor is made of a concrete slab, while the other floors have varying heights and formats. Plywood is used for walls and shelving, and gives the home an uncomplicated feel. The architects were inspired by Alfred Loos's ideas of Raumplan—ordering and sizing rooms in a home according to their function. Thus, there is a balance kept between open social spaces and cozier nooks for quiet reading—and, of course, there is a place for drumming.

KOERFER HOUSE, 1967

Ascona, Switzerland

MARCEL BREUER

Jacques C. Koerfer was an entrepreneur and art collector, who numbered Old Masters, Impressionists, and Modernist works by Picasso, Braque, and Léger among his collection. In 1963, he and his wife Christina commissioned Breuer to build a 14,000-square-foot (1,300-square-meter) residence for them on the shores of Lake Maggiore. Invisible from the road—one needs a boat to see it—this home has a bunkerlike aesthetic that is typical of brutalist houses. On the lake-facing side, it opens up completely to nature with a cantilevering terrace. Breuer embraced the sculptural qualities of concrete: to him, it was useful not just structurally but also aesthetically, for he could use it to make stunning visual and plastic effects, as seen in his treatment of the external stairways and the interlocking planar surfaces of the house.

DELBIGOT RESIDENCE, 1973

Villeneuve-sur-Lot, France

JEAN NOUVEL

Almost submerged in turf, this house was designed by Jean Nouvel when he was twenty-eight. At the time, Nouvel was studying in Paris and rebelling against the way Le Corbusier was presented as a model to follow. While working in the studio of his professors, Paul Virilio and Claude Parent, Nouvel had the chance to design the Deligot Residence, along with two associates, François Seigneur and Roland Baltera. A two-story house, its roofs are pitched at various conflicting angles, the floors slope, walls are angled, and windows incline—it seems an attack on similarity and neutrality. From a distance the house appears as a confluence of ramps and concrete blocks. Its plan, however, is conventionally rectilinear: a living room, dining room, and office dominate one side of the house; kitchen, bathroom, and hallway occupy the other.

LA ROCA HOUSE, 2006

Punta del Este, Uruguay

MATHIAS KLOTZ

Boxlike houses have held ongoing fascination for Chilean architect Mathias Klotz, and he has constantly striven toward defining a new poetics of the form. Klotz's portfolio is also built around the idea of belonging, as it reflects a strong sense of a place. The project at La Roca (The Rock), in a fishing village near Maldonado, had a challenging plot that sloped along both its length and width. Klotz's pragmatic response was to design two separate cuboid dwellings, primarily in ipe wood and exposed concrete, one for living and one for sleeping, connected by a glazed walkway. Outdoor spaces— a deck on the lower floor, a courtyard nestled between the walkway and the two boxes, and patios underneath the two volumes—are interwoven within the arrangement. The roofs of both structures are covered in succulents to retain heat in winter.

BOMBALA FARMHOUSE, 1997

Bombala, New South Wales, Australia

COLLINS AND TURNER

Sited high on the remote Monaro Plains of New South Wales is a prefabricated hillside retreat for a farmer and his family, designed by Penelope Collins and Huw Turner. They are former colleagues of Norman Foster, himself a well-known advocate of prefabrication. The farmhouse's pure abstract forms create a sculptural presence in the landscape. Two volumes, one a living area and the other for sleeping—inspired by Marcel Breuer's concept of binuclear houses—interlock neatly. The skillion roofs and galvanized steel cladding reference local farm buildings. Everything is pared down, functional, and simple. Ornament is rejected in favor of lines and forms that allow the bush and farmland to be the main focus. The Bombala Farmhouse yields to a Modernist European tradition, but it is also unmistakably Australian in its functionality.

TURBULENCE HOUSE, 2005

Abiquiu, New Mexico, USA

STEVEN HOLL

This part of New Mexico is Georgia O'Keeffe territory, and it is here, too, where artist Richard Tuttle and poet Mei-mei Berssenbrugge bought a plot and commissioned Holl to build them a guest house and owners' retreat, which is constructed adjacent to the adobe courtyard houses built by the clients. The arched structure consists of thirty-two prefabricated metal sections, the largest of which weighs a ton, bolted to flexible metal ribs; the home's curving, segmental metal-panel skin appears to be stitched together like a quilt. It is not comfortable. Tuttle has said: "It's too hot in the summer, too cold in the winter." Rather, it is a form of desert visual poetry. The "Turbulence" in the name references the wind that howls through its center, carving a curving void not dissimilar to an inverted desert canyon, within which is the entry door.

CASA BALDI, 1961

Rome, Italy

PAOLO PORTOGHESI

Bound to the earth by its use of native tufa (a soft, porous rock) interspersed with thin lines of red brick, the Casa Baldi has been described as an "archaeological fiction" due to its self-conscious allusions to other architectural periods, especially the Baroque. A precursor of postmodernism, the house loosely borrows the forms of Guarini or Borromini, with its undulating concave curves—with gaps in between for windows overlooking the River Tiber. Three spatially fluid stories are separated by a string course cornice: a lower ground floor, a grander main level, and a smaller second level much like the roof terraces of the Modernists. Portoghesi advocated an architecture that "listens" to its site: "Listening architecture tends to put the building in key with the place, making it grow out of the place like a plant."

CASA GHAT, 2015

Cachagua, Chile

MAX NÚÑEZ ARQUITECTOS

Casa Ghat is positioned on a steep bank along the coast of the Pacific, and the design of the structure and its spatial arrangement are heavily influenced by this unique topographical condition. The large, concrete roof canopy, angled parallel to the slope of the site, functions as an enormous staircase descending to a viewing platform above the main living area. The irregularly shaped concrete columns that support the structure help delineate the internal spaces of the house and at the same time the spectacular views of the water. Inside, the organization of the house is less a series of rooms than a topography of varying levels and heights. Two private zones on the upper level, their exteriors clad in wood, emerge from the roof plane like dormers, providing additional means of access to the terrace below.

HOUSE IN VORDERTAUNUS, 1992

Vordertaunus, Germany

STUDIO GRANDA

The large house that Margret Hardardottir and Steve Christer—collectively known as Studio Granda—built in Vordertaunus is really two buildings: a timber-clad pavilion and a red-painted box. Taken together, the two create a rich mix of spaces—those in the former are light and airy (the roof terrace, in particular, has fantastic views), the latter are more intimate and cozy. It is typical of this young Icelandic practice to approach a house design in this way. Its best-known work to date—the competition-winning design for the city hall in Reykjavik (1992) which launched their career—has an equally complex combination of private and ceremonial spaces. In the face of much contemporary architecture, which emphasizes the need for light and open-plan living, Studio Granda recognize that people need different spaces to suit their moods.

DESERT COURTYARD HOUSE, 2014
Scottsdale, Arizona, USA

WENDELL BURNETTE ARCHITECTS

Scottsdale is known as "the West's most Western town." In the Sonoran Desert, outside the city, amid an arid boulder-strewn landscape, is this luxurious, monolithic courtyard house. Situated on a rocky outcrop at the lowest part of a development, it is overlooked by other properties. Its exterior was therefore designed to make the house merge with its surroundings, and it is built from rammed earth from the site excavation, concrete, glass, and weathered steel. "We wanted the house to recede like a shadow in the landscape," said the architect. Living areas face the central courtyard, which is filled with trees, saguaro cacti, and rocks, which in effect brings the desert into the structure itself. At night, glass disappears, and the milled steel ceilings appear to blend with the inky sky outside.

HAUS L, 1996

Weerberg, Austria

MARGARETHE
HEUBACHER-SENTOBE

Margarethe Heubacher-Sentobe is an Austrian architect who studied at Vienna's Akademie der bildenden Künste before working at Loch, Tuscher and Norer in Innsbruck, establishing her own practice in 1978 in Schwaz. She is best known for her 2003 design of the Carmelite convent in Innsbruck, although she generally specializes in unusual private dwellings, like House L. Clinging to a perilous slope, this raw concrete house is made of three stacking sections, funneling outward like the body of a camera. Lateral and frontal glazing gives the house an extraordinary transparency as well as vertiginous views. A small projecting balcony allows the inhabitants to further immerse themselves in the alpine landscape. Space for two grand pianos, one at the front of the house, one at the rear, is prioritized.

WARNER HOUSE, 1957

New Canaan, Connecticut, USA

JOHN JOHANSEN

The pink stucco-clad Warner House, which is also known as the Bridge House, straddles the Rippowam River in a wooded area of Connecticut. Johansen uses the bridge as a metaphor for a liminal place: one which is suspended in time and space. With an H-shaped plan, four square pavilions, each with a different function, connect to a central living and dining pavilion at the heart of the house. Underneath this part, the river flows, bisecting the living room in such a way as to align perfectly with a vault in the ceiling. Luxuriously burnished in gold leaf, the ceiling vaults over time have turned a rich shade of copper, on which the river's reflections dance and shimmer. The house also features eight gilded gargoyles. Johansen has said that the Warner House "most elegantly interpreted the Palladian ideal."

T HOUSE, 2005

Graz, Austria

FEYFERLIK FRITZER

This sylvan family house is situated in a former park in Graz, on a grassy, southwest-facing slope. The aim of the design, by architect Feyferlik Fritzer, was to meet the client's needs for space without excessive deforesting of the site. The house is constructed around and between the trees—at one location, a trunk pierces the roof overhang and becomes part of the building. Eastern, southern, and western elevations have floor-to-ceiling glazing to maximize views. The interior makes generous use of wood on floors, walls, and ceilings. The children's area is reached by a separate entrance, which means the residence contains flexible spaces which can be used independently of each other. Black steel clads the north wall so that it shimmers with reflections of the trees, stressing the importance of nature to this project.

VIEW HILL HOUSE, 2012

Yarra Valley, Victoria, Australia

DENTON CORKER MARSHALL

Overlooking the magnificent land of Yarra Valley, in the winemaking region of Victoria, View Hill House sits on a hilltop above a vineyard. The elementary geometry of the two long rectangular structures, one perched atop the other at a ninety-degree angle, creates a pure architectural object in the landscape. The dramatic design is a two-story family residence; the bottom volume is clad with pre-rusted steel, while the smaller top volume incorporates black aluminum sheets. Each end of these volumes offers a clear view of the surrounding landscape through floor-to-ceiling square windows, which allow natural light to flood the interiors. The interior design features polished concrete floors on the ground level, while much of the top level is covered in more modest chipboard; rough, natural materials are used throughout the house.

SOLO HOUSE II, 2017
Matarraña, Spain

OFFICE KERSTEN GEERS
DAVID VAN SEVEREN

This vacation home is part of an on-going project of contemporary resort prototypes commissioned by French developer Christian Bourdais. Situated in Cretas, a forest area in the mountainous region of Matarraña, the Solo House II is built on a natural plateau, which gives a 360-degree panorama of the surrounding wilderness. The concrete foundation is a circular catwalk, of sorts, and a flat roof functions as a shelter for the outdoor patios. Rooms inhabit four sections; stretches of metal mesh curtain slide on the outer edge of the circle, allowing the living areas to fully open to the outdoors. The house is self-dependent: Photovoltaic panels, water tanks, and generators are contained within sculptural roof volumes, which have been painted in a gradient effect by artist Pieter Vermeersch. It is at once discrete and imposing, luxurious, and austere.

DUNE HOUSE, 2011

Thorpeness, England, UK

JARMUND/VIGSNÆS ARKITEKTER & MOLE

Crowned with an eye-catching black, faceted upper story, which resembles a hat, this seafront holiday house by Norwegian architecture firm Jarmund/Vigsnæs, in collaboration with British studio Mole, references the vernacular of the gabled barns and sheds found in the area. The ground floor is entirely clad in glass, emphasizing the floating appearance of the top floor. The upper level, which is clad in dark-stained timber, is organized as four triangular rooms beneath a steeply pitched, zigzagging mansard roof, decorated with contrasting metallic panels and featuring irregular window openings. In 1910 the architect, barrister, and playwright G. Stuart Ogilvie planned Thorpeness as a fantasy holiday retreat; this contemporary home, just south of the village, has been built with a sense of homage to Ogilvie's vision.

HOUSE IN MATHILDENHÖHE, 1901

Darmstadt, Germany

PETER BEHRENS

With its sensuously elongated gables, Behrens' house in the Darmstadt artists' colony betrays his connection with Jugendstil. Yet its stark colors, lack of ornament, and compositional discipline foreshadow the rational synthesis between design and industry he would achieve later. In 1901, Behrens was transforming himself from a Jugendstil artist into an architect via interior decoration. Following the philosophy of Nietzsche, he and his contemporaries believed that art could address the huge social and economic questions of modern life which characterized Wilhelminian Germany. In 1907, Behrens was appointed as architect of AEG, an electrical company. His work melded design and industry, setting the tone for the Deutsche Werkbund and starting a theme which reverberated throughout the twentieth century.

MOORE HOUSE, 1962
Orinda, California, USA

CHARLES MOORE

Charles Moore invested the many houses he designed for himself with his original and often whimsical artistry. Despite tight budget constraints, this small house near San Francisco—one of his early projects—displays all the artistic invention for which he became renowned. Two groups of enormous, solid timber Tuscan columns form the dramatic primary structure and planning nucleus of the house. Above each cluster (one defining the living space, the other a sunken bath), a pyramidal skylight floods the interior with light. The juxtaposition between the heavy structure and the lightweight external envelope is emphasized by the fact that the walls never meet at the corners, where you would expect to find structural support. Instead, sliding glass panels open the building up to views of the oak forest beyond.

EICHLER HOME, 1950s & '60s

San Francisco Bay area, California, USA

JOSEPH EICHLER

Well-designed, inexpensive modern homes were hard to find in the San Francisco Bay area before businessman-turned-building contractor Joseph Eichler built his first housing development in 1950. While living in a rented Frank Lloyd Wright house, Eichler conceived of a new breed of affordable housing that would not sacrifice quality for cost. Although modest in scale, Eichler Homes have impressive features, such as open floorplans, high ceilings, exposed redwood beams, and underfloor heating. Bedrooms and bathrooms are often on the street side to reinforce the privacy of the main living space. The characteristic rear glass facades create continuous views overlooking the yard and remain one of the most popular features of the homes. Today, more than 2,700 Eichler Homes still survive in the Bay area.

HIGH AND OVER, 1929

Amersham, England, UK

AMYAS DOUGLAS CONNELL

Connell's first major commission has three cubic wings forming a Y-shaped plan around a hexagonal hall, and is orientated to make the most of spectacular views. Corridors are almost completely eliminated and spaces flow elegantly yet informally into one another. The lengthy bands of windows and rooftop sun terrace show the influence of Le Corbusier, but the house also reflects the interest in Classical proportion of both architect and client, Bernard Ashmole, director of the British School in Rome where Connell studied. High and Over has been viewed both as the last great British country house and as the first Modern house in the English countryside. In 1933, Connell established a partnership with Basil Ward and Colin Lucas. As Connell Ward Lucas they built what are considered by many to be the best interwar Modern houses in Britain.

SUMMER HOUSE, 1937

Gudmindrup Lyng, Denmark

ARNE JACOBSEN

The shed roof which gently attaches itself to the large wall, the outdoor fireplace which hangs on the chimney, the picture window and the patio, all exemplify the informality and relaxed relationship to the outdoors of much Scandinavian architecture of this period. Even the potentially monumental curved wall, which organizes the more casual components of the architect's own summer house, is broken down through texture and horizontal articulation. But the whiteness and proportion of the house set it apart from nature, and this tension makes it a pivotal design in Jacobsen's career. One of the key figures in the development of Scandinavian Modernism, he was educated to balance new techniques and functions with tradition and culture, and later on his houses were closely attuned to a northern European climate.

SHEARER'S QUARTERS, 2011

North Bruny Island, Tasmania, Australia

JOHN WARDLE ARCHITECTS

Melbourne architect John Wardle has a farm on Tasmania's North Bruny Island (human population: 620; sheep population: thousands, 1,800 on his farm alone). He designed this compact, modern, low-lying hut, formed from traditional corrugated iron, next to a sublime, green-blue inlet. It's for guests, sheepshearers, and staff from his practice, who come to work the land or plant trees. The hut's west end begins as a skillion roof, evolving into a flat gable to the east, creating an intriguing shift in geometry. All of the living spaces are pine clad, referencing the wood used for apple crates (apples are also farmed here); a haul of ancient crates, found in an old orchard, was recycled and used to clad the bedrooms. Rather than being a pastiche of the vernacular architecture, this building is community- and future-driven.

W.I.N.D. HOUSE, 2014

North Holland, The Netherlands

UNSTUDIO

Located on the outskirts of a Dutch village and close to the sea, the W.I.N.D. House is backed by a wooded area and fronted by an open expanse of polder landscape. Each of the four facades curves inward to form a series of distinct, petallike wings. These recesses are visually connected to each other through their view lines, which cross at the heart of the home. Heat gain is reduced through the use of tinted glass on the entirely glazed front and rear facades. There are smart features: a comprehensive home automation system enables integrated control of the electrical systems, including solar panels and mechanical installations. Complete control of this smart residence is provided by way of a touch screen in the living area, while decentralized devices give dedicated control per room.

LIFT, 2010

Sendai, Miyagi, Japan

APOLLO ARCHITECTS
& ASSOCIATES

The black cantilevered volume of the LIFT house appears to have risen from underground. The client, a family of five, wanted a home that would be efficient in its use of space: open and optimistic. The interior spaces are predominantly white; the black exterior is meant to delineate the dramatic forms that are typical of the surrounding residential buildings. Living spaces are arranged across two floors, and are centered around a courtyard, which provides light and air circulation to rooms otherwise closed to the outdoors—the angular facades of the house are largely devoid of windows or glazing. To accommodate the client's love of movies, there is a soundproof room located on the ground floor. A street-facing balcony is fronted with timber louvers for privacy, while allowing for views of the street from the kitchen.

HOUSE ON THE TOP, 2016

Curanipe, Chile

MUTAR ESTUDIO

The young Chilean firm Mutar Estudio designed this elegant and lofty summerhouse for two couples in the small coastal town of Curanipe, a popular holiday resort. The idea was that both couples could use the house together at the same time, while still being able to maintain a feeling of privacy and separation. Mutar designed three pavilions elevated on a podium facing out over the Chovellén River. The central pavilion is a shared living area, while the couples' own private areas are to the left and right. The units are parallel to one another but staggered to accommodate the diagonal slope of the plot. Although the House on the Top is sited some distance from the sea, each pavilion is compensated with floor-to-ceiling windows, which frame the wide landscape views, like large paintings.

SHINGLE HOUSE, 2010

Kent, England, UK

NORD ARCHITECTURE

Environmentally protected due to its special fauna and flora, the unique pebbly spit of Dungeness in Kent is a windswept, filmic place in the shadow of a nuclear power station. The name of this four-bedroom house references the stony beach it stands on, but also its wooden cladding of black-stained cedar shingles. The residence comprises a group of three volumes (two single-story and one double-story) connected by glazed corridors; the configuration mirrors that of the house and sheds that the home replaced on the plot, and its stark geometric form echoes the tarred fishermen's huts of the area. The living-room glazing folds back to open up to the landscape; more glazing folds open to provide access to an inner courtyard, which becomes a warm and sheltered spot on sunny days.

VILLA HOHENHOF, 1908

Hagen, Germany

HENRY VAN DE VELDE

In 1906 Karl Ernst Osthaus proposed to build Hohenhagen, an artist colony of sixteen villas, in a wooded plot in Hagen. Hohenhof—characterized by its traditional materials—would be his family home and the nexus of the estate. The house features blue-black stone, which blends with black basalt lava and bluish slate. Like William Morris and British exponents of the Arts and Crafts movement, van de Velde believed art was not something one hung on the walls, but an approach to be applied to all objects. This house was a complete artistic environment for which he designed not just the building, but also all the furniture, light fittings, and cutlery (he even designed his wife's clothes). A triptych of ceramic tiles by Matisse decorates the internal "winter garden." Osthaus died in 1921 at age forty-six, and the colony was never completed.

CASA MALAPARTE, 1938

Capri, Italy

ADALBERTO LIBERA

In building the interwar Casa Malaparte, Rationalist architect Libera, together with his client, the writer Curzio Malaparte, reinforced something of the myth of the writer in his solitary study on this bare rock of his Capri island exile. Conceived as a simple stone house, the design was soon developed to incorporate a broad, ritualistic flight of tapering steps that lead to the plain roof terrace. This detail ties the house to its rocky setting, demonstrating how a building can be treated as a geographical accent. This relationship with nature is continued inside by a series of small windows framing intense views along the dramatic coastline. Although more modern than classical in its architectural heritage, the house manages to evoke an antique ruin; indeed, it was built almost in sight of Tiberius' Villa Jovis which had, at the time, just been excavated.

NEUENDORF HOUSE, 1989

Majorca, Spain

JOHN PAWSON & CLAUDIO SILVESTRIN

A shimmering swimming pool projects from the terrace of this holiday house for a German art dealer, out toward the horizon and the rugged red landscape of southern Majorca. The house stands like a square medieval fortress, rendered with local earth-colored stucco, with local limestone used throughout for the floors and for massive tables, benches, and basins. Despite its geometric purity, the whole composition is conceived to allow architecture and nature to interact and enhance one another. The outer walls have only narrow openings, and the brightness of the interior courtyard contrasts with the calm of the interiors. Pawson and Silvestrin are the primary exponents of architectural Minimalism, eliminating all ornament from their architecture, but creating a sense of austere luxury through the use of expensive natural materials.

LINEAR HOUSE, 2009

Salt Spring Island, British Columbia, Canada

PATKAU ARCHITECTS

Salt Spring Island sits within the sheltered inland Salish Sea. Linear House—one continuous volume 276 feet (84 meters) long—faces an avenue of mature Douglas fir trees, through which the sea can be glimpsed, on one side; the other side overlooks an orchard. Everything about this house is geared toward the panoramic vista: as the inhabitant walks through its rooms, the framed view shifts. Seventy-eight-foot (24-meter) lengths of floor-to-ceiling glazing can be pushed back to open up the house, transforming it into an outdoor pavilion—in this state, its form embodies a shelter rather than a proper house. The Linear House's subdued charcoal-colored exteriors contrast strikingly with the pale wood, light-filled interior. Set amid the trees, its form is mysterious and abstract, described by the firm as "a dark, stealth-like figure."

SHELL RESIDENCE, 2008

Karuizawa, Nagano, Japan

ARTECHNIC ARCHITECTS

It is as if a gigantic shell had been dropped by a bird in the middle of a wooded grove. This two-story vacation home by Artechnic is situated in the forest of Karuizawa in the Nagano Prefecture. Its curving, horizontal forms contrast radically with the verticality of the trees. The use of reinforced concrete makes the building better able to handle the demanding climate—humid and cold—than some nearby residences that are deteriorating. From above, the home is J-shaped. By raising the house 5 feet (1.5 meters) above the ground, the architects avoided the soil's dampness and allowed room for a custom-built heating system. Cocoonlike and minimalist inside, the emphatic lack of straight lines or sharp angles provides a sense of escape and relief from the constraints of urban living.

HEARST CASTLE, 1947

San Simeon, California, USA

JULIA MORGAN

"La Cuesta Encantada," the Enchanted Hill, was how William Randolph Hearst described this audacious retreat he had built overlooking the Pacific Ocean. Resembling a flamboyant Spanish mission church, the castle appears to be designed as a set for the Hollywood stars who were among Hearst's frequent guests. Built over 20 years, the complex grew to 130 rooms, with decorative elements and artworks drawn mainly from southern Europe and inserted into a reinforced concrete structure. Besides the main house, there are guest cottages, greenhouses, outdoor and indoor pools, and a pergola encircling the hill for more than a mile. Tycoon Hearst was the inspiration for the movie *Citizen Kane*, and his castle, in turn, a model for Kane's fictional house, Xanadu. Morgan studied at the Ecole des Beaux-Arts in Paris—the first woman to be admitted.

HOUSE IN NIPPONBASHI, 1992

Osaka, Osaka Prefecture, Japan

WARO KISHI

This minimal, "pencil" dwelling stands strong as a white geometric gem in this traditional urban district of Osaka. A steel-frame structure, with prefabricated concrete side panels, supports three compressed lower floors and an upper dining space, with a high ceiling, and adjacent open-air roof garden. The street facade's steel louvers, screens, and stairs act as a semi-permeable interface between the city and the living-work spaces beyond. Originally schooled in architectural history, Kishi practices in the more traditional city of Kyoto and draws from many sources, including the California Case Study houses and the *sukiya* aesthetic, as expressed in the seventeenth-century Katsura Imperial Villa. This house is one of Kishi's many urban townhouses designed as prototypes of a new, aesthetic, industrial vernacular architecture.

BREUER HOUSE NEW CANAAN I, 1948

New Canaan, Conneticut, USA

MARCEL BREUER

The controlled simplicity of this Breuer house—essentially two rectangular forms, one of natural timber cantilevered over another of white-washed concrete—demonstrates his rational design method. Such a disarmingly simple organization, stemming from a very straightforward idea, is characteristic of both Breuer's architecture and his furniture designs, such as his tubular chrome and black leather Wassily armchair (1925). Built into a hillside, this house is relatively small but very open, with large banks of windows and an overhanging balcony suspended by thin steel cables; the concrete base, which was covered by fieldstone in the 1980s, contains a workshop. Breuer's attention to detail, seen in the diagonal boarding of the cantilevered portions of the house, help to define each element's importance.

VOLGA HOUSE, 2009

Tverskaya, Russia

PETER KOSTELOV

On the banks of the Volga, this dacha (country home) is clad in a patchwork of differently slatted wood panels. Their complementary rhythms soften the heavily massed superstructure. The weekend house is designed to accommodate two couples and their grown-up children, some of whom need work space, so it is a flexible and roomy dwelling. Constructed on an existing foundation, the architect built upward to get the maximum amount of space—and also to get the best views of the Volga from a higher vantage point. He also built outward, creating a new open wooden terrace and shed. Kostelov considers the design to be suggestive of Soviet-era dachas, which were built piecemeal and used whatever materials became available, thereby demonstrating the lives of the buildings and their changing owners.

HEMEROSCOPIUM HOUSE, 2008

Madrid, Spain

ENSAMBLE STUDIO

Like a fragmentary game of Jenga, this house in Madrid is created from a sequence of additions and subtractions which shape a bold domestic composition. Its structure is organized in a helix formed of seven key elements: three over-scaled I-beams, two trusses, and two U-shaped concrete channels. Organized by open-planned square floors, the house is delineated by the colossal elements. The structure was assembled on site in only seven days. Walls of glass enclose the heavy, mute spans, and frame views across the district of Las Rozas. A lap pool is suspended one floor above ground level in a cantilevered channel accessed from the master bedroom, with a larger swimming pool below. Perched on the top of an I-beam, a rough-hewn boulder block appears to balance precariously. In truth it acts as a hefty counterweight.

HOUSES OF THE HORIZON, 2009

Zapallar, Chile

UNDURRAGA DEVES ARQUITECTOS

This pair of clifftop houses was designed as a retreat from Santiago. They are a virtuoso exercise in horizontality; each is a bridgelike structure, a two-story dwelling resting on twin orthogonal stone volumes. The houses are in staggered formation, sharing one of the stone volumes as a support. In both, ground-floor living areas—lounge, studio, and dining room—are completely transparent, arranged along a corridor, adjacent to which is a void serving as an undercroft barbecue area. The upper floor, with six bedrooms and a principal living room, is similarly amply glazed, providing views over the sea. The roof is a flat plane held between two massive parallel concrete beams. It overhangs the lower level, and provides sheltered sun terraces. Two lap pools are tucked behind each of the houses and abut the hillside.

CUBIST HOUSE, 1991

Yamaguchi, Yamaguchi Prefecture, Japan

SHINICHI OGAWA

This glass cube house, in a typical residential neighborhood in Japan, stands in stark contrast to its surrounding chaotic urban context. However, the simple repetition of the steel grid facades, each one divided into thirty-six square glass panels, emphasizes the house's neutrality, and the images reflected on the glass surface help its substantiality to vanish into its surroundings. Within the cube is an inner, more private solid structure, set back behind the glass wall, containing most of the accommodation. A gallery and a continuous ramp which connects to the first floor where an open workspace is situated create a buffer between the two. The overall effect is that of a jewel placed in a free-flowing setting. The contradictory features of the structure's mass suggest an unconventional relationship between a house and its urban context.

VILLA SHODHAN, 1956

Ahmedabad, India

LE CORBUSIER

Le Corbusier's commission to design the new city of Chandigarh brought with it projects for clients in other Indian cities. Corbusier created the Mill Owners' Association Building (1951) for Surrotam Hutheesing, as well as this villa. It is presided over by a large rectilinear cantilevered concrete roof; its slab appears to float, simply supported by pilotis and minimal shear walls to the rear. Equally audacious was the exposed principal elevation, protected from sun and rain by enormous concrete brise-soleils with living spaces recessed behind this interstitial zone. The large openings allowed for cross-ventilation and mimicked established Gujarati colonnades that assuaged climatic extremes. Characteristic Corbusian elements abound, such as an internal ramp, and intense color applied to raw shutter-marked concrete.

TOHMA HOUSE, 2009

Hokkaido, Hokkaido Prefecture, Japan

HIROSHI HORIO

Part of a farm in rural Hokkaido, Tohma House was conceived for a small creative farming family whose love of nature extends to all which they endeavor. The residence, perched on a terrace above planted fields, is clad in black-painted timber clapboard. This emphasizes the solid forms of the multiplaned roof and prismatic tower, while also serving to conserve and absorb heat during the cold winters. Interior spaces are layered atop one another and culminate in a light-filled, fully functional barn attic. The program is organized around the wood-burning fireplace, which sits at the rear of the ground-floor great room and functions as the primary source of heat throughout the winter. Interior framing has been left exposed, and the unfinished appearance adds to the functional, utilitarian aesthetic of this farm residence.

POLE HOUSE, 1978

Fairhaven, Victoria, Australia

F2 ARCHITECTURE

This small weekend retreat is perched 42 feet (13 meters) above the endless blue and gold of Fairhaven Beach off the Great Ocean Road in Victoria. A similar wooden structure had been there since 1978, but, crumbling as a result of the damp sea air, it was demolished to make way for this sophisticated reincarnation. Reached by a slender concrete bridge from the road, the simple, boxlike dwelling, with a pyramidal roof and clad in metal at its rear, is supported on a massive pylon buried deep into the hillside. Accommodations are minimal—one bedroom, one bathroom within a wooden drum, and an open-plan living and dining area—and do not detract from the main event: the views. From its elevated position, the full-height glass walls retract, opening the interior to the elements.

VENICE HOUSE, 1991

Venice, California, USA

ANTOINE PREDOCK

Despite its urban locality, this beach house in Venice, California, demonstrates Predock's landscape-based architectural approach. A glistening black granite reflecting pool provides a cool stillness between the house and the pedestrian boardwalk below, and acts as a conceptual bridge between the house and the sea. Predock believes that views should be framed rather than panoramic; here, a one-ton giant pivot window focuses views of the Pacific Ocean, and allows the smells and sounds of the sea to enter the house. It is powder-coated red, the same color as the Japanese flag; the architect has said he was thinking of the ritual importance of the sunrise in Japan. A large roof terrace has views in all directions: toward the beach, the ocean, LAX flight paths, and the hills of Palos Verdes and Malibu.

STUDIO HOUSE, 1930
Meudon, France

THEO VAN DOESBURG

This studio house is the culmination of van Doesburg's attempts to translate the tenets of Neo-Plasticism—a Modernist preoccupation with shifting volumes and sliding planes—into a built form. The artist/architect was best known as the incessant polemicist of the De Stijl movement, whose early endeavours at architecture were compelling, unbuilt constructions of intersecting planes of primary colors, similar to the paintings of his colleague Mondrian. However, in this, his last built project, he moved toward a more objective, technical solution. Traces of the kinetic spirit of van Doesburg's early compositions can still be seen here—the two cubic volumes seemingly pulling apart, the studio in the upper cube and the living quarters in the lower one. Also, his usual palette of primary colors is retained in the doors and openings.

SHAPESHIFTER, 2018

Reno, Nevada, USA

OPA

This Shapeshifter house was built for two art dealers specializing in contemporary works from the American West. OPA (Ogrydziak Prillinger Architects) explain that their sensitivities toward art needed to be reflected in the design: both the feeling of being of the moment and up-to-date, and of the West. Describing the desert as a "space of ambivalence and uncertainty," they devised a home that changes form depending on the angle it is viewed from. Starting with the site, they shaped it into "anticlines and synclines, dunes and blowouts," from which the final shape of the house emerged. Surrounded by mounds of earth, the house is literally dug into the landscape. The exterior is formed of long zinc panels and sheaths of glazing which connect, creating a multifaceted, mutable, and jewellike house.

CROFT HOUSE, 2013

Inverloch, Victoria, Australia

JAMES STOCKWELL ARCHITECT

Inverloch is a small seaside town on the Victorian coast of Australia; this house is on an exposed part of the coast nearby. This house "turns its collar up" to prevailing easterly winds without completely shielding itself from their effect. Shaped like a sand dune and inspired by the oscillating sine curve, the tapered exterior allows for peripheral views from within, and disguises expansive interior space. Inside, gently curving walls direct the eye outward, creating a lens bisected by the ocean. Its corrugated zinc skin references local farm architecture; and there is no heating or cooling. Much like the water in its midst, this building implies movement. The architects believe that there is an instinctive bond between people and other natural systems, and this building engages the natural elements. It is a home that embraces its landscape.

VILLA BERTEAUX, 1936

Uccle, Brussels, Belgium

LOUIS HERMAN DE KONINCK

Inspired in his early days by the Art Nouveau architecture of fellow Belgian Victor Horta, de Koninck's interpretation of the Modern style was formally more creative than that of many of his European contemporaries. This is shown at the Villa Berteaux in the interplay between horizontal and vertical windows; this playful composition also borrowed the porthole windows and metal handrails from ship designs, a favorite Modernist source. De Koninck was renowned for his technological innovation; he introduced the exterior reinforced concrete wall to Belgium, for example. This home displays his mastery of construction techniques with smooth, rounded corners, and elegantly composed volumes. De Koninck also designed the CUBEX kitchen, a series of modular components that could be assembled in various configurations to fit a client's needs.

FAMILY HOUSE AT THE EMPORDÀ, 1973

Mont-ras, Spain

RICARDO BOFILL TALLER DE ARQUITECTURA

This vacation home, built for the architect's father, is composed of seven individual sections orientated toward a pool. The central, red pavilion encloses the dining area, while other more private sections contain the living space, bedrooms, and kitchen. The house sits on a rectangular platform, yet Bofill has adopted a deliberate defunctionalizing aesthetic that emphasizes geometrical organization, proportion, and enclosure. The house seeks to embrace its natural setting; the high windows in the interior courtyard mimic the pointed cypress trees and the brown earthen tones of the walls visually connect the house to the rock outcroppings that surround it. Bofill is perhaps better known for his huge housing complexes, but this private house shows his ability to work on an intimate scale using both modern and classical historical precedents.

H HOUSE, 2011
Budapest, Hungary

BUDAPESTI MUHELY

The H House is a contemporary interpretation of the traditional Hungarian peasant house. The deconstructed design is distinctive for its steeply gabled symmetrical massing. The majority of the structure is skinned in wooden shingles, while the northeast facade is clad with vertically oriented black metal panels, creating a textured aesthetic program. The house is built along a simple interior plan, and divided down the middle by a passageway from which rooms extend on either side. Each room, designed as modules, is precisely 129 square feet (12 square meters), as the client believes that this size is an ideal configuration for their home. The living area, which combines four modules, extends the full length of the house; its double-height section continues up into the eaves.

BRADLEY HOUSE, 1910

Madison, Wisconsin, USA

LOUIS SULLIVAN

One of the most influential forces of the Chicago School, Louis Sullivan designed some of the finest houses in turn-of-the-century North America. In the Bradley House, his most complex and mature domestic work, Sullivan employed a cross-shaped plan using the entry vestibule as the symbolic heart of the house. From this space, the two axes radiate out into a sequence of rooms. On the exterior, the dominant volume containing the main living and sleeping areas is intersected by a smaller block, which is more expressively articulated and features a semicircular study. Any impression of heaviness is alleviated by cantilevered porches at each end of the building. The house is a vibrant example of Sullivan's philosophy that form should follow function, an approach he always inflected with his sensitive employment of Beaux-Arts organic ornamentation.

ESTERS HOUSE, 1930
Krefeld, Germany

LUDWIG MIES VAN DER ROHE

In late 1927 Mies was commissioned to design two houses side by side for two clients: the art collector and textile manufacturer Hermann Lange and his managing director, Josef Esters. Both homes are blocky, L-shaped, and large in scale. The clients resisted the open-plan layouts of Mies's Brick Country House (1924) and Wolf House (1927). The steel-frame structure with brick cladding gave flexibility on where windows could be placed—but Mies envisioned more floor-to-ceiling glazing than the clients wanted. While the clients were less adventuresome than Mies had hoped, the Krefeld houses are significant in another way: they demonstrate Mies's dexterity in gradually transforming given norms—his ability to give shape to new architecture incrementally by transforming conventions rather than projecting an ideal.

PINK HOUSE, 1979

Miami Shores, Florida, USA

ARQUITECTONICA

This is a house of layers, pink upon pink, with gradations from powder-pale to vibrant rose. Designed by Bernardo Fort-Brescia and Laurinda Hope Spear, the husband-and-wife team behind Arquitectonica, this house grew to define a new era in Miami, ending the long period in which architects spurned the vibrant colors of the tropics. The Pink House is an unconventional Modernist form that draws on the dual traditions of Art Deco and the Bauhaus, both predominant in Miami; its primary building materials are stucco-clad concrete inset with glass block. The setting, on the shore of Biscayne Bay, reinforces its tropicality, as does the central feature, an internal swimming pool that runs along the entire north–south axis of the building. Founded in 1977, this firm gained a reputation for its daring use of color and boldly innovative geometric forms.

RUDIN HOUSE, 1997

Leymen, France

HERZOG & DE MEURON

Herzog & de Meuron designed this family dwelling which appears to mimic the iconic child's drawing of a house. However, while the simple form appears familiar, there are many details that confound expectations. For example, the "front door" is accessed via a flight of steps from underneath the building, and the pitched roof joins the walls smoothly with no protective overhang. Although cast in concrete, the house appears, contradictorily, to float above its site. The Swiss architects, inspired by the fact that, unlike Switzerland, French building laws do not require a cellar, determined to clear away all that normally anchors a building to the ground. The flat plinth rests on concrete pilotis, projecting beyond the ends of the house to reinforce its lightweight appearance. With its sliding floor-to-ceiling windows, the house opens up to the surrounding fields.

STREET-PORTER HOUSE, 1988

London, England, UK

CZWG

The spiky, angular forms of Piers Gough's house for Janet Street-Porter are purposely designed to look like its owner—a well-known TV presenter with distinctive spectacles. It is an eclectic, referential building with an upside-down *piano nobile*—the main reception rooms are one floor down from the top. The triangular-windowed, rooftop eyrie is a study entered via an external spiral staircase—to keep work and home separate—and is vaguely suggestive of a bohemian Paris garret. Below, diamond "spectacle" screens enclose one balcony, while another balcony projects from the kitchen to hold up the end of a table. The bedroom takes up the entire first floor, while a staircase rises through the house, with a mesh-floored dining room projecting over it. The brickwork gets lighter in color the higher up the facade: a visual trick copied from New York.

LUCKY DROPS, 2005

Setagaya, Tokyo, Japan

ATELIER TEKUTO

The sliver of land this house was built on is awkwardly shaped, but that made it inexpensive, allowing a young couple to buy it. The tapering plot meant that the maximum width possible for any house would be just 6 feet (2 meters), but the couple embraced the challenge. Including a basement and making the exterior skin—fiberglass-reinforced plastic panels—as thin as possible maximized the internal space. The plastic panels also gave the structure a delicate translucency, and its arching form enclosed in supporting ribs is like an upended boat. Yamashita has said that the house "looks like a chopstick." The name Lucky Drops comes from a Japanese proverb that says the final leftovers of a portion can bring a fortune. In this case, it was the leftover land that provided the couple with a home.

STEVENS HOUSE, 1968

Malibu, California, USA

JOHN LAUTNER

Built in the late 1960s, this home is sublime for its wavelike form, which rises up among a parade of other, more conventional beach houses in Malibu. The proposal was to build a five-bedroom and -bathroom home on a tight plot: only Lautner said that it was possible. His solution was avant-garde: two concrete half catenary curves supported by a structure of fourteen steel I-beams. The interior is clad with cedarwood planking. Lautner was apprenticed to Frank Lloyd Wright after graduating and became the first of the Taliesin Fellows, before going on to set up his own practice. He revered Wright, although the architectural critic Henry-Russell Hitchcock considered that his work could "stand comparison with that of his master." Other celebrated Lautner houses include the Sheats House (1963) and the Chemosphere residence (1960).

NEW HOUSE, 1986

Sussex, England, UK

JOHN OUTRAM

Like a set design for Mozart's *The Magic Flute*, Outram's New House suggests strength and power, with a touch of melodrama. The entrance courtyard has virtually no windows, drawing attention to the wide central doorway, while the armillary sphere seems to indicate a place for some kind of ritual enactment. Although they may not be explicit, the house carries many levels of symbolism through which Outram likes to bring his work to life. This is expressed in the hierarchy of materials which includes colored concrete. The interior has many finely crafted details, creating patterns in floors and on walls, continuing the richness of color from the exterior. Outram is no ordinary postmodernist, but an original contemporary architectural thinker, with an ability to communicate successfully to non-architects through his unrestrained decorative designs.

BELL BEACH HOUSE, 1965

San Diego, California, USA

DALE NAEGLE

In the mid-1950s, Sam Bell, of Bell's potato chips, wanted to add a guesthouse to his summer home atop the cliffs overlooking Black's Beach. The site included the cliffs themselves, so Naegle, whose mentors included William Perreira and A. Quincy Jones, produced an eccentric solution, designing a pavilion on the beach which could be reached by a funicular railway. Visitors would trundle down the cliff to enter the mushroom-shaped home via a drawbridge, where they would be greeted by panoramic views of the Pacific. The beach was accessed by a spiral staircase down the pavilion's "stalk," which at high tide was lapped by waves. The house's second owner installed walls around it and reconfigured the interior. Unfortunately, the clifftop home was demolished in 1990, and the railway is no longer functional.

CUBE HOUSE, 2000

Ithaca, New York, USA

SIMON UNGERS & MATTHIAS ALTWICKER

Located in a field outside the university city of Ithaca in upstate New York, the Cube House reduces the elements of "home" to their essential state. Devoid of ornament, it is inescapably a statement of principles. Simon Ungers, who designed the home with Matthias Altwicker, calls it a "block." Formed of precast concrete blockwork, the house is arranged over two floors. A studio takes up the entire ground level, with living quarters positioned above. A roof terrace, open to the sky, is accessible from either floor via an external staircase. The seemingly random pattern of window openings in the blockwork is a visual break from the house's rationalist bent. The Cube House, with its perfect regularity and rigor, neither responds to nor ignores its rural setting. It is like a functional earthwork, a sculpture that provides shelter.

HOLMAN HOUSE, 2004

Sydney, New South Wales, Australia

DURBACH BLOCK ARCHITECTS

Located in Sydney's Dover Heights, Holman House perches precariously over the edge of a 230-foot (70-meter) cliff above the Tasman Sea. The curvilinear form of the building, inspired by Pablo Picasso's 1928 painting *The Bather*, fluidly expands and contracts to direct views of the surrounding cliffs and across the water in all directions. Inside, the living spaces have been adapted to the meandering perimeter, its apertures positioned in response to the movement of the sun throughout the day. Living and dining areas cantilever over the water, supported by a series of slender columns. This volume is anchored to a base constructed from rough stone, designed to appear as though it were an extension of the rock face below. These walls continue around the property, converging to create a series of terraces that accommodate gardens and a pool.

MIMA LIGHT, 2011

Viana do Castelo, Portgual

MIMA HOUSING

Inspired by the Minimalist cuboid sculpture of artists such as Donald Judd and John McCracken, MIMA Light is the simplest, most affordable building offered by Portuguese company MIMA Housing, which specializes in prefabricated dwellings. The sleek, modular home is completely made and assembled at a factory, ready to be transported to its site. It can be bought in two lengths—29½ feet and 39½ feet (9 meters and 12 meters)—and used as a holiday home, weekend retreat, or office space. Resting on a mirrored base, the structure seems to float above the ground—a neat visual trick. The interior layout can be open plan or divided into rooms; glazing can be positioned flexibly as well. Outside, it is clad with aluminum panels, while pinewood lines the interior walls.

CASA M-LIDIA, 2002

Montagut i Oix, Spain

RCR ARQUITECTES

Pritzker Prize–winning RCR Arquitectes—founded by Rafael Aranda, Carme Pigem, and Ramon Vilalta—designed this low-budget, containerlike stainless-steel house for a couple in the village of Montagut amid a volcanic landscape of striated black and red earth. Cantilevering off a gentle slope, it features an underground garage with a single story for living and sleeping. A block with living and eating areas connects to two L-shaped wings on either side: the gaps between each of the three volumes create miniature courtyards. The central block is contained and secure, but there is a sense of openness, flow, and permeability. The sculptural house has been described as having a "Zen essence of the organic and of geometry"—rooted in its terrain, in dialog with nature rather than trying to camouflage itself.

MAISON DE JEAN PROUVÉ, 1954

Nancy, France

JEAN PROUVÉ

Over four months in 1954, Prouvé, his family, and some friends built this house out of lightweight stock elements purchased at Maxéville—Prouvé's recently closed prefabricated house factory—on a slope overlooking Nancy. Both the structure and furniture are made up of standard components, able to be carried by only two people; the piecemeal effect is due to a desire to experiment in the use of various materials. Prouvé is now regarded as one of the most influential designers of the early Modernist movement and particularly of innovative housing solutions: mass-produced, demountable, and transportable houses whose angles, volumes, and materials gave a sober elegance, halfway between craft and industry. This house was classified as a historical monument in 1987, and was a blueprint for many prefabrication projects that followed.

LITTLE BIG HOUSE, 2010

Fern Tree, Tasmania, Australia

ROOM 11 ARCHITECTS

This two-story pine-clad dwelling in Tasmania is a rectangular box that is simple, but interesting for a number of detail-oriented decisions. Extensive research was devoted to finding exactly the right position for the house to maximize views while maintaining privacy, but finally the "worst" part of the site was chosen—near the entry road—to allow views over mossy vegetation and provide a garden. The boxlike structure steps down the slope at two levels, cantilevering outward over the hillside. While some glazing provides delightful outlooks, other areas of the facade are covered in translucent polycarbonate, playing with ideas of the expected and unexpected in such a house. It is interesting programmatically too; living space, apart from the kitchen, bathroom, and toilet, is entirely reconfigurable and flexible.

CRESCENT HOUSE, 1997

Winterbrook, England, UK

KENNETH SHUTTLEWORTH

The main space of this house is the garden room, a single volume accommodating all the communal activities of Shuttleworth's young family: cooking, eating, relaxing, and playing. However, despite this open planning, the building is also restrictive; for example, the concave glass wall bathes the room in light, but has no sections which open to allow immediate access to the garden, so as not to detract from the simple geometric form. Shuttleworth wanted a home which was "spacious and airy yet utilitarian and functional," and not "lavish, profligate, or precious." All the surfaces are white, apart from the raw concrete of the chimney and end wall. Color is provided by furnishings and objects which are changed over each season: towels, cushions, bedlinen, tablecloths, and vases are blue in winter, yellow in spring, green in summer, and red in autumn.

SCULPTURED HOUSE, 1963

Genesee Mountain, Colorado, USA

CHARLES DEATON

Sitting atop Genesee Mountain, the Sculptured House was planned to be Charles Deaton's own residence. Its unique elliptical form placed the project within the tradition of sculptural Expressionism and provoked controversy. "People aren't angular, so why should they live in rectangles?" said Deaton. But for the architect, the house was less about Futurism, and more aligned with ancient structures which united earth and sky. The project was abandoned before it was entirely completed due to cost, but it entered the public consciousness in 1973 when it was used in Woody Allen's film *The Sleeper*. Deaton died in 1996; the house was bought in 1999 by John Huggins, who had it extended according to Deaton's plans. Now a private residence, the Sculptured House is on the National Register of Historic Places.

HAYES RESIDENCE, 2014

Berkeley Springs, West Virginia, USA

TRAVIS PRICE ARCHITECTS

A building created with simplicity and sensitivity can, in the right conditions, result in a powerful space. The Hayes Residence, sited above the bed of a stream in a forested park near Berkeley Springs, is surrounded by oak and birch trees. The architects have fully embraced this arboreal environment by leaving some of the growth undisturbed: the house actually wraps around a few trunks, which, left exposed behind glass, create the impression of posts supporting the large beams of the vaulted ceilings. The main house is narrow and unobtrusive, lying low in the woodland. The foundation meets the ground in only two places; the structure of the building hinges from two large columns. Patinated copper, slate tiles, and almost continuous walls of glass compose the building's exterior. The house is in quiet dialog with the landscape it is a part of.

ROCK HOUSE, 2009

Vestfold, Norway

JARMUND/VIGSNÆS ARKITEKTER

The site of an existing summerhouse on a rocky promontory in Vestfold, on the shore of the Oslo Fjord, has been transformed into a strikingly different take on the coastal retreat. The new home's shape, height, color, and materials are sympathetic to the local landscape; it is low-lying, echoing the gently curving rock forms nearby, and built partly on the stone walls of the old house. Stone that was blasted out of the cliff was also recycled by incorporating it into the design. Jarmund/Vigsnæs shaped the house to follow the contours of the rocks it hugs, and voids have been cut into its facade to provide wind-shielded outdoor spaces. Kebony wood was chosen for the cladding, to weatherproof the home against the hammering it will inevitably receive from the elements in this exposed location.

NEUTRA VDL, 1932

Los Angeles, California, USA

RICHARD NEUTRA

In 1931 Neutra received a gift of $3,000 from industrialist Cornelius Van Der Leeuw toward designing a new house. Neutra purchased land overlooking Silver Lake Reservoirs and built a radically Modern home and studio for just $8,000. Boxlike, with repeating windows and a thin, flat roof, it introduced a new, more European Modernism to American residential architecture. His wife, Dione, said in 1970, "Every step from room to room, stairway up and down, is an aesthetic and artistic experience, which I have the good fortune to enjoy." Built in 1932, it burned down in 1963 but was re-created by Neutra and his son Dion on the original footprint. Some say the restoration was heavy-handed; others insist that introductions, including a floating staircase and sun louvers, added to the lightness of the Modernist structure.

TREE HOUSE, 2009

Separation Creek, Victoria, Australia

JACKSON CLEMENTS BURROWS

The location is spectacular, high above the Great Ocean Road and Bass Strait, but this two-bedroom, two-story home is at heart a modest and pragmatic solution to a challenging plot. It has a look of the vernacular "fibro" shacks common during the 1950s Australian housing boom, using two-tone green cement sheet panels to create a harmonious visual fit with its natural environment. Wooden battens covering the joints between panels complete the retro appearance, and will silver over time. The steep slope, landscape controls, and landslide potential meant that Jackson Clements Burrows had to work on a limited footprint. Using volumes that cantilever in four different directions addressed this, resulting in a cruciform, treelike building. The distinctive design branches out from the standard "glass box" cliffside retreat.

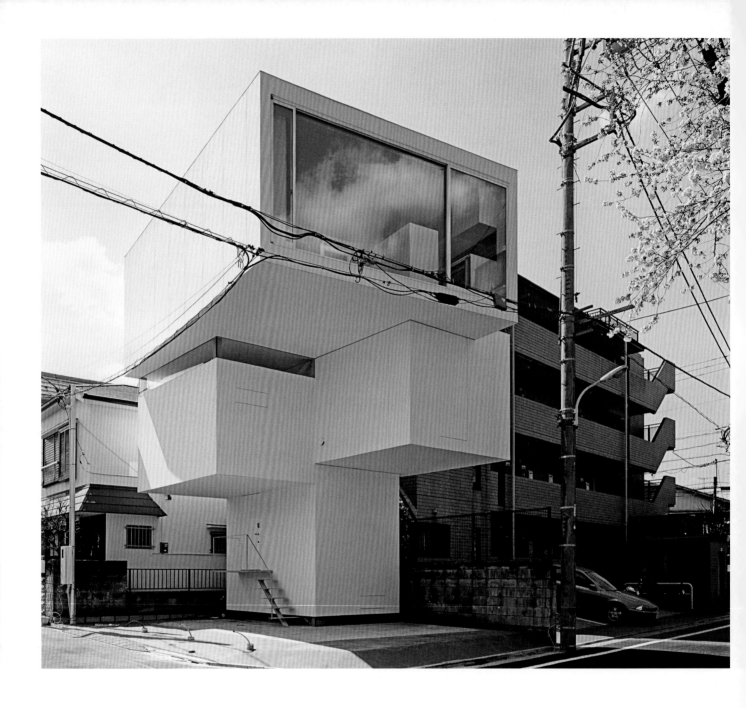

ON THE CHERRY BLOSSOM HOUSE, 2008

Itabashi, Tokyo, Japan

A.L.X.

This house is designed to get the best possible view of two cherry trees' springtime clouds of pink blossoms. Junichi Sampei of A.L.X. (Architect Label Xain) has gained a reputation for creating sublime homes in tricky urban spaces, many of which are in Tokyo. Each of this building's three floors branches out, treelike, from a central spiral staircase. The first floor, essentially a cube, has one room. The second floor, another cube, consists of two bedrooms and a study. The third, a larger oblong box, is the main open-plan living space, which pivots away from the rest of the block to allow as direct a view of the trees as possible. Sampei has created for his clients an urban tree house of sorts, and, in the right season, inhabitants can enjoy the vista of the blossoms from the comfort of their home.

DROP IN HOUSE, 2005

Long Island, New York, USA

MB ARCHITECTURE

A bold synthesis of old and new, the Drop In House shows how prefabrication can be used to make a clever extension to an older building. In this case, the existing house in Southampton, Long Island, was shingle-clad and in a traditional style. Project architect Maziar Behrooz designed a boxy prefabricated volume which was literally "dropped in" to the original house by crane. The extension features a roof terrace, accessed by a turretlike stairwell. Thus, the house is a quirky blend of different-shaped volumes: cylinder for the stairwell, cuboid for the extension, and the archetypal arching gables of the shingled house. Prefabrication is a passion for MB Architecture—the practice also designed the insta_house, which is a prototype prefabricated house, in 2009. That project is now in production.

CHMAR HOUSE, 1989

Atlanta, Georgia, USA

SCOGIN ELAM & BRAY

As it soars skyward, this house exults in nature while, at the same time, showing deference to it. It is at once a tour de force and yet, somehow, quite unassuming. The Chmar House sits on a site next to a nature preserve; thus the bucolic nature of the setting in the rolling wooded Atlanta countryside is well protected. The actual placement of the house was selected after a tree fell here, naturally providing a clearing. The house is raised above the ground on treelike columns to cause as little disruption to nature as possible; the living areas form one wing, and the guest quarters another. The design draws inspiration from Japanese architecture and ritual (the clients are practicing Buddhists), so that the spaces unfold as a ceremonial passage. The interiors are clad in birch and plywood panels, with windows of varying shapes and sizes.

BAVINGER HOUSE, 1955

Norman, Oklahoma, USA

BRUCE GOFF

Bavinger House was one of an extraordinary series of experimental houses designed by Goff. The house was self-built by the sculptor-client, Bavinger, with his family and his students. Sited on a small, rocky ravine—the bridge helped to stabilize the house. A single mast, made of two oil-drilling pipes and old biplane wires, supported a copper-covered timber roof over a single, continuous spiral space. The kitchen and bathroom were tucked into the core of the spiral. Protruding into the main space was a series of open pods for dining or sleeping, with separating curtains. A rubble-stone wall wrapped around this form. While Goff's work had moved on from his early influences by Frank Lloyd Wright, he continued to develop the use of site, materials, and program as key elements. Despite the house's architectural significance, it was demolished in 2016.

DARVISH RESIDENCE, 2004

Nour, Iran

POUYA KHAZAELI PARSA

The Darvish Residence, designed by young Iranian architect Pouya Khazaeli Parsa, is located in a densely developed resort on the southern coast of the Caspian Sea. The site has no view of the ocean at ground level; instead, views are had from private L-shaped roof gardens, accessed via a wide external ramp, which is an extension of the domestic space. The house is approached from the southeast corner, where a staircase leads to a sizeable entrance terrace on the first floor. From the exterior, this terrace is the focus of the building, creating a void at the corner of the three-story volume, and distinctive for its bright orange painted surfaces. The interior spaces are organized to provide different levels of privacy. For example, the kitchen and dining room buffers the master bedroom from the rest of the house.

SMALL HOUSE, 2000

Tokyo, Tokyo Prefecture, Japan

KAZUYO SEJIMA

The metaphor which underpins Small House's design is that life is fluid and ever changing. On a tiny plot in Aoyama, an affluent area of Tokyo, the family home occupies just 828 square feet (77 square meters). Essentially, it is a steel-framed four-story tower whose surfaces have been twisted on the diagonal to create a dynamic geometric shape. Inside, it is a normally functioning home, with each level dedicated to a different function: master bedroom, second bedroom, bathroom, and living area, the form and size of each story adjusted according to need. A single spiral staircase corkscrews through each of the floors, creating subtle subdivisions of space. On the exterior, irregular glass and mesh facades interlock to create a zigzagging frontage that suggest perpetual movement and flow.

VILLA IN THE FOREST, 1994

Tateshina, Nagano, Japan

KAZUYO SEJIMA

The client of this house, a scientist who also deals in paintings, commissioned this as a second home to accommodate artists visiting from abroad. The house consists of two circular walls that each have different centres; the outer wall delineates a profile of the house while the inner wall divides the house into two parts, an atelier and a dwelling space. Sejima, whose earlier projects emphasized a continuity between inside and outside, wanted to create a self-contained continuity within the building's substantial walls. The continuous space between the two circular walls gently diminishes and extends in width and height, demonstrating her almost obsessive preoccupation with circular movement. Here Sejima offers a simple yet evocative response to the forest environment and her client's practical requirements.

LOOSDRECHT LAKE HOUSE, 2011

Breukelen, The Netherlands

2BY4-ARCHITECTS

Squeezed onto an island not much wider than the house itself, Loosdrecht Lake House is located in the midst of a Dutch nature reserve. The small vacation cottage is constructed on a *legakker*, a manmade topographical feature in which lake islands are formed by excavating surrounding peat. The house is clad in black-stained timber clapboard referencing the previous structure it replaced and the traditional black barns that were once a common feature on the Dutch landscape. Additionally, the somber exterior palette lessens the cabin's visual impact on its natural environment. The one-level dwelling is divided into two sections by a slightly raised floor level. One section contains the kitchen and storage areas; the other encloses the sleeping and living zone, which have wide views over the lake and the forest beyond.

LANARAS WEEKEND HOUSE, 1963

Anavyssos, Greece

NICOS VALSAMAKIS

The generative principle for the design of this vacation house was that of obtaining unimpeded views from the main living area toward the Saronic Gulf, above which the house is located. The living and dining rooms are situated in the glazed volume contained between the two concrete slabs cantilevered out over the sloping site. The slabs, supported by slender steel columns, extend to create a large covered terrace. The design of the house is a sensitive response to its context by establishing a dialogue between the internal spaces and the setting, and is, in many ways, reminiscent of the 1950s Case Study houses of California. Functionalism, compositional clarity, and clear references to context are typical qualities of the architecture of Valsamakis, as is his attempt to adapt Modernism to Greek regional culture.

BASS RESIDENCE, 1976

Fort Worth, Texas, USA

PAUL RUDOLPH

Paul Rudolph had visited Frank Lloyd Wright's Fallingwater shortly before designing this magnificent residence; Fallingwater had been a lifelong obsession of his, and its influence shows in the strong horizontality and interlocking volumes of the Bass House. It is Rudolph's most ambitious domestic project. The street-facing elevation is almost blank, and concealed by a thick grove of trees; on the garden side, the facade opens up into a symphony of white-painted steel planes and cantilevering volumes. A floating canopy stretches between the two upper wings of the house, truncating their outward thrust and framing a three-sided courtyard. Rudolph described the Bass Residence's origins by explaining, "[The] ideal of weight and counterweight, similar to the movement of the human body, became the genesis of this house."

HOUSE VI, 1975
Cornwall, Connecticut, USA

PETER EISENMAN

House VI is a famous example of taking architectural theory to its limits. When designing this post-and-beam Connecticut home, Eisenman began with a grid. Within that grid he created a design that mostly ignored the users' needs and instead represented the design process itself. Different stages of thought and changes of mind were incorporated into the final structure; elements of architectural theory were physically represented, with little regard for functional purpose. Thus, there are curious features in the final grid structure: an upside-down red staircase denoting the house's axis; a column hanging over the dining table that separates diners, and a glass strip bisecting the entire bedroom, forcing a couple to sleep in separate beds. Clients Richard and Suzanne Frank adapted to living there while acknowledging its challenges.

ESHERICK HOUSE, 1961

Chestnut Hill, Pennsylvania, USA

LOUIS KAHN

In this building, Kahn endowed what is, in effect, a small suburban house—constructed in the stuccoed, timber-frame vernacular of countless such houses—with something of the monumentality of ancient architecture. He achieved this using two means. First, a plan of almost Palladian simplicity: two long, deep rooms either side of a staircase hall, one side a double-height living room, the other a dining room with a bedroom above it, and a service block to the side. Second, the facades onto the street and garden have deep alcoves—solid with bookshelves on the street side, and largely open on the garden side. Solid timber doors to the garden, set back the whole depth of the reveal, alternate with wider bays of glazing set flush to the outer face of the wall, forming full-height bay windows.

ALONSO-PLANAS HOUSE, 1998

Barcelona, Spain

CARLOS FERRATER

Crisp forms, geometric regularity, and sharp details reveal an architecture of restrained poetic formalism that is Carlos Ferrater's hallmark. By using a visually simple but conceptually complex set of interlocking spaces, he seeks a richness of experience through simplicity of means. The house sits perpendicular to the contours of a sharp slope, with three stories of accommodation overlooking the valleys of Barcelona and the sea. Two low, L-shaped wings extend to form a tunnel entrance to one side and a submerged art studio on the other, lit by a strip of clerestory windows. Large expanses of white walls block out the bright sun, with horizontal scoring on the surface to break the visual monotony. The overall effect of the white planes under the intense blue sky is an ambiguity of scale and materials, adding a surreal effect to an otherwise quiet rationality.

HOUSE IN ITSUURA, 2014

Kitaibaraki, Ibaraki, Japan

LIFE STYLE KOUBOU

This house in Ibaraki Prefecture uses the timber from the cleared area of woodland it is built on. A predominant part of the angled house is supported on two organic-style pillars, and the rest of the structure is embedded in the hill. There are two distinct wings, which form a V-shape: living spaces are in the longer wing, while the shorter has a range of versatile spaces for sleeping, studying, or play. Interiors are timber-clad, and the facade features external louvers which provide light yet maintain privacy, and also regulate temperature. The dwelling's horizontality contrasts beautifully with the verticality of the supporting pillars and trees. As the wood weathers, it will become more visually integrated with its natural surroundings. Following construction, the architects planted sixty trees to help regenerate the surrounding landscape.

TWO-FAMILY HOUSE, 1992

Athens, Greece

DIMITRIS ISSAIAS &
TASSIS PAPAIOANNOU

The brief for this residence, situated at the foot of Mount Pendeli in Athens, was to provide accommodation for three generations in two separate units. Entered via a small courtyard, the house is developed over three levels; the grandparents inhabit the courtyard level, while the parents and children live on the upper two floors. The design is based on an analysis of the everyday activities taking place in a family home. There are internal and external vertical routes through the building, which playfully exploit the relationship between inside and outside spaces. The use of materials, such as exposed concrete for the columns of the visually dominant structural grid and blockwork for the walls, illustrates the architects' concern with the use of building techniques which could be executed by local builders.

HOUSE AT SANTANDER, 1983

Santander, Spain

JERÓNIMO JUNQUERA &
ESTANISLAO PÉREZ PITA

Sitting atop a flat rise, boldly overlooking the Santander port, this house design clearly embraces the International Style. Junquera and Pérez Pita have drawn their inspiration from the industrial glass building style developed by Mies van der Rohe, specifically from his Farnsworth House (1951)—the prototype for glass houses. The exterior expresses strict geometry in its modular component parts. Walls have been turned into window panels, thus exposing the traditionally private life of the home to the public. Virtually all structural and interior design components are visible. The high ceilings and glass walls of the living room flood the home with light, and add to the overall open feel of the home. The architects have fully adapted what would traditionally be industrial building materials and design for this residential habitation.

VIEW HOUSE, 2009

Rosario, Argentina

JOHNSTON MARKLEE & DIEGO ARRAIGADA ARQUITECTOS

Surrounded by trees and sited beneath huge Argentinian skies, the View House embraces its name. A design arising from an American–Argentinian collaboration, it is part of the Kentucky Club de Campo development on the outskirts of Rosario. This house evokes an overwhelming sense of space—both inside and outside. Views are opened up by oversized windows, but this is not a goldfish bowl; they are strategically placed. The building's form is the antithesis of the conventional development house with front and back facades. Corners and edges have been sliced away to make scooped, angular, and tilted planes. Inside, those subtractions result in a changing diorama of curves, recesses, and surprising views. The home's rough concrete shell has been made using local techniques, yet interior surfaces are polished and smooth.

HAUS L, 2003
Bregenz, Austria

PHILIP LUTZ

As cable cars sail overhead, this house, high up on the Pfänder mountain in Bregenz, has fantastic views over the city and Lake Constance. When architect Lutz bought this plot to build a home for his family, there was an existing house on the site. The old dwelling was fully demolished, with the exception of a cellar, and Lutz designed this wooden prefabricated house to sit on top of it. The bold, prismatic forms of Haus L would seem to be inspired by brutalism, yet they have been cleverly rendered in wood, not concrete. The exterior is completely covered in the traditional shingles of the region. Bedrooms are situated on the ground floor, with the living area, marked by extensive glazing, above; there is a large sheltered terrace on the south side, and a bridge connects the house to the forest behind.

SCHRÖDER HOUSE, 1924

Utrecht, The Netherlands

GERRIT RIETVELD & TRUUS SCHRÖDER

The open-plan spatial organization of this house was remarkable for its time. The first floor was occupied by a large living and dining area, with sliding panels for partitioning off smaller rooms. It was also innovative in its use of huge windows, strong blocks of color, and built-in furniture. The design was developed by the client, Truus Schröder, in collaboration with Rietveld, as an expression of her desire for a house where she could live closely with her children and entertain a constant flow of visitors and liberal ideas. Rietveld started his career as a furniture designer with links to the radical Dutch De Stijl art movement. This house is celebrated as the first architectural embodiment of De Stijl principles of color and abstraction, with its white and grey intersecting planar walls and colored railings, and is a landmark in the history of modern house design.

HOUSE BEFORE HOUSE, 2009

Utsunomiya, Tochigi, Japan

SOU FUJIMOTO

The House Before House is a dwelling that conflates interior with exterior space. Designed with the premise that people naturally live interstitially, as opposed to only indoors, the house—rather experimental in its conception—operates as a village of sorts. Individual rooms, separate from one another, are nevertheless united by staircases and courtyards to form a spatial continuum. This labyrinthine series of structures represents a search for harmony between the natural and the manmade. This traditionally Japanese concept of living allows for the house to boldly stand out against its surroundings while incorporating, at various scales, elements of the natural environment. The house intelligently plays with habitual preconceptions of what defines a dwelling, to become far more than a series of interconnected rooms.

BARON HOUSE, 2005

Skåne, Sweden

JOHN PAWSON

New York–based creative director Fabien Baron bought this property with the idea of building a secluded vacation house for his family. The scheme which emerged from the design process preserves the general footprint of the original agricultural buildings, which were cleared away: four single-story wings set around a courtyard. The exterior vocabulary is pared down to white rendered walls, corrugated roof pitches, and frameless glazing in full-height openings, with corresponding sliding timber shutters. Inside, white plaster walls rise to meet a lofty geometry of pitched planes, and generous apertures open the interior to the landscape. Consistent with a form predicated on an agricultural shed, the construction was kept as simple as possible. Baron House is stark, ethereal, and stripped of ornament, a place to empty the mind.

BELLTREES HOMESTEAD, 1907

Scone, New South Wales, Australia

JOHN PENDER

Henry Luke White, the grandson of an English immigrant farmer, was a renowned ornithologist who made significant contributions to the knowledge of Australia's unique bird species. In 1907, he commissioned John Wiltshire Pender to build Belltrees Homestead, one of the finest Australian Federation-style homes in New South Wales. This style is a derivation of the English Edwardian style with its Art Nouveau influence, adapted to reflect the Australian climate and availability of building materials. Belltrees features symmetrical facades with shady verandas on both ground and first level. The richly decorated balustrades incorporate timber and "lace" ironwork, typical of this style. The interiors, in contrast to the dark colors of the preceding Victorian taste, were light and airy, and provided a dramatic backdrop to the grand baroque timber staircase.

PLANAR HOUSE, 2018

Porto Feliz, Brazil

STUDIO MK27

Situated within a softly undulating green landscape close to a lake, this house designed by Studio Mk27 is distinctive for its massive turf roof; supported on pillars and bearing walls, but no beams, the concrete slabs of the roof have been envisioned by the architects as a fifth facade of the building. This radical exercise in horizontality extends past the living spaces and creates vast sheltered verandas. The house is formed of two adjacent orthogonal volumes, one for the gym, service areas, TV, and playrooms, and the other for five bedrooms; living rooms are at both extremities. The home's surrounding glass doors can be slid completely open, creating a giant terrace. Providing a sense of enclosure, a snaking lattice-pattern brick wall surrounds an entrance garden area on one side of the house.

HOF, 2007

Skagafjörður, Iceland

STUDIO GRANDA

Located in the north of Iceland, Hof is the home of Icelandic film director Baltasar Kormákur and his wife, Lilja Pálmadóttir. The one-story house is located within the shadows of a farmhouse that Pálmadóttir used to stay at as a child—and which she now owns. Hof is a series of connecting volumes that project and recess in the landscape. Using concrete, stone from the nearby mountain, and sheer cedar from British Columbia, it has a low impact on its surroundings, which is characteristic of the work of Studio Granda. Basalt rock found when digging foundations is used for flooring and kitchen countertops, and telegraph poles salvaged from the site are used as a sun/privacy screen for south-facing windows. The concrete walls insulate the Hof house extremely well, as do the stone floors.

SCOPE, 2012

Shimada, Shizuoka, Japan

MA-STYLE ARCHITECTS

In this project, the architect wanted the client, a longtime resident of the area, to reconnect with the sweeping views from a hillside down over the Makinohara plateau, a region rich with many tea plantations. The area of the plot that could be used was restricted because of the risk of landslides. The design solution employed three interlocking trapezoidal forms, resulting in a sculptural, abstract composition. The main elongated volume, glazed at one end like an enormous viewfinder, houses the living and dining rooms; inhabitants ascend to this upper level via a slender spiral staircase, into a space of geometry, light, and natural vistas. Its front end rests on a trapezoidal platform; at the other end, it penetrates a much larger tilting block accommodating two bedrooms upstairs, and a bathroom on the ground floor.

HOUSE IN KOHOKU, 2008

Yokohama, Kanagawa, Japan

TORAFU ARCHITECTS

This unconventional home is located on a hill in the city of Yokohama. The plot faces north and the neighboring homes are two-storied; rooflights ensure the house receives good natural light. The roof consists of three truncated pyramids of reinforced concrete. Inside, the sloping lines of the ceiling make subtle demarcations of space throughout the house: ceiling arrises split internal spaces into the living area, sleeping area, and so on. "We aimed to make the exterior and interior appear as two sides of the same object," the firm explained. This creates a homely interior—tent or trulli-like, resonating with primeval notions of home and protection. The use of *béton brut* on the exterior speaks of humility and a lack of pretension, but the House in Kohoku certainly makes no attempt to conform to the local environment.

MAISON DRUSCH, 1965

Versailles, France

CLAUDE PARENT

The tilt of this Modernist, rectilinear house at a 120-degree angle is intended to blow apart the restrictions of straight-lined, static architecture. Designed in 1963, the Maison Drusch was the first house built by the radical French architect, Claude Parent. Parent advocated rejecting the conventional form of buildings to open up new freedoms: roofs tilted for walking over; walls only built in order to stop people walking into others who are sleeping. But the house was also designed as a comfortable home for an engineer and his family, who originally wanted a traditional building. The house is composed of two separate parts, the tilted bedroom block anchored by the three-story living accommodation block. Although it is a pragmatic realization of an idea, the overwhelming impression of it falling over—with its suggested dynamism and instability—remains.

VALLEY HOUSE, 2015

Dolomites Mountains, Italy

PLAN BUREAU

This conceptual house has been designed by Ukrainian firm PLAN bureau as a family holiday home. It is intended for a mountain location—hence the unusual, twin-peaked shape—but Kuvika said it could be used in any rural situation. Its design is reminiscent of Andrew Geller's Pearlroth House (1959) in Westhampton Beach, New York, although that project features a symmetrical "double-diamond" form, whereas the Valley House is asymmetrical. It is designed to be simple to install and easily transportable. Living space is on the lower level, while bedrooms are in the boxy upper volumes. The house's shape allows panoramic views. It is clad in pine both inside and out, and weatherproofed on the exterior. The Valley House is an intriguing reimagining of the archetypal countryside cottage.

MELNIKOV HOUSE, 1929

Moscow, Russia

KONSTANTIN MELNIKOV

A remarkable fusion of two masonry cylinders, Melnikov's house and studio, in its traditional street setting, is a strong statement which recalls formal Constructivist experiments. Its interior arrangements, however, demonstrate how awkward such forms are to adapt for occupancy, even for the bohemian lifestyle of an artist. The spaces are most successful on the upper floor, when the whole form is incorporated, or where freestanding screens do not compromise the volume. Underneath are irregularly shaped storage rooms with hexagonal windows, a visual incongruence from the mystic components of Russian Constructivism, alongside revolutionary and *sachlich* elements. Somehow, during the New Economic Policy, Melnikov managed to build this extraordinary house and remain in it, throughout the Stalinist terror, for almost fifty years.

JOSÉ DA SILVA NETO'S HOUSE, 1976

Brasília, Brazil

JOÃO FILGUEIRAS LIMA

Influenced by the sensual shapes of Oscar Niemeyer's postwar buildings, this residence is constructed entirely out of concrete. It was designed by the Brazilian master João Filgueiras Lima. As in several other of Lima's projects, he lifted the principal volume of the house above the ground. The main living space is situated on the second floor, supported by four strong, curved arches, creating both the primary constructional feature and aesthetic feature of the project. The layout is based on a simple rectangle with linear terraces the length of the house on both sides. The north facade is adjusted by an oval-shaped staircase tower, which serves as an entry point to the house. A ceramic tiled wall below the house defines the outdoor space; the tiles were created by Brazilian sculptor and painter Athos Bulcão.

ALEXANDER STEEL HOUSES, 1962

Palm Springs, California, USA

WEXLER & HARRISON

These steel houses on a remote tract of desert land near Palm Springs were designed by Modernists Richard Harrison and Donald Wexler, who had visions of their prototype going into mass production: "We were hoping it would be like the first Ford," said Wexler. Perfect for weathering extremes of heat and cold, steel was—at the time—relatively cheap. Forty units were planned, each with an identical floor plate, with variations in room configuration, glazing, and roof design. Modular panels—consisting of a steel skin, insulated with gypsum and fiberglass—were prefabricated in Los Angeles and assembled on site. Disastrously for Harrison and Wexler, steel prices rocketed, and only seven of their homes were built. Renovated in the 1990s, these are now considered classics, combining economy and simplicity with a Palm Springs panache.

SUMMERHOUSE LAGNÖ, 2012

Lagnö, Sweden

THAM & VIDEGÅRD ARKITEKTER

This Swedish summerhouse designed by Tham & Videgård Arkitekter is situated in the Stockholm archipelago, built atop a concrete plinth and facing a bay. It appears from a distance like a collection of vernacular, gabled-roof homes. Constructed in concrete, the outer shell was cast in situ; a faint checkerboard pattern has been impressed into it, and the texture of the wooden molds is visible—creating a visual echo of the archetypal wooden summer hut or boathouse. The main house and guesthouse are separated by a glazed, pitched canopy, which frames the seascape beyond. Inside the main house, the pitched roof translates into ceilings of varying heights, a device used to define different areas for cooking, eating, and relaxing in the open-plan space. A detached block, similarly built from concrete, contains a sauna.

NEW HOUSE IN RANZO, 2012

Sant'Abbondio, Switzerland

WESPI DE MEURON ROMEO ARCHITEKTEN

This concrete home hugs the mountainside and overlooks Lake Maggiore. It is designed for two people and their guests. The three-story cuboid house is simple in form—a straightforward tower—and connects, on the valley side, to a series of steps leading down to a parking area. It is built of pale *béton brut*, carefully selected to complement the local stone of nearby dwellings. Irregularly placed windows give the facades an abstract character and add pattern and variation to the block. Openings are positioned to maximize views of the water, woods, and mountain. Inside, occasional use of stone detailing in the polished concrete floor creates a connection between the artificial and the natural. This minimalist home is suffused with a sense of wellbeing—the architects describe this as life lived amid "the poetry of nature."

CARLSON-REGES RESIDENCE, 1996

Los Angeles, California, USA

ROTO ARCHITECTS

Formerly the machine shop for the city's first power station, this Neoclassical pavilion has been converted into an unusual urban residence near downtown Los Angeles. Surrounded by railyards and a major freeway, it presented the architects with the challenge of providing a hospitable living environment, as well as a semi-public garden gallery. Gathering inspiration and a variety of materials from the client-builder's own scrapyard, RoTo successfully combined the simplicity of the existing structure with a series of large-scale interventions that work both with, and against, the logic of the original 1920s building, creating infinite opportunities for unexpected juxtapositions. Perhaps the most inventive addition is an old steel gasoline tank, found on the site, that was cut in half and welded together end-to-end for use as an elevated lap pool.

PETAL HOUSE, 1982

Los Angeles, California, USA

ERIC OWEN MOSS

Located just north of the Santa Monica Freeway in Los Angeles, one part of this house dates back to the 1950s—a one-story home with a detached garage. The architects explored possibilities for extending the home and in the process questioned everything with the owners, including "What is a window?" "What is a door?" and "What is a wall?" The house's name comes from its most prominent addition, the shingle-clad master bedroom with an exploded pyramidal roof—its four sides open up at asymmetric angles as if it were a flower opening to the sun. Space for working—an office/studio above the garage—was included, which was unusual at the time. The final forms which were chosen are ultimately postmodern deconstructions of elements of the house typology, and materials, forming a quirky whole.

VANNA VENTURI HOUSE, 1964

Chestnut Hill, Philadelphia, USA

VENTURI, SCOTT BROWN, & ASSOCIATES

The flat, overstated, metaphorical facade of this house has become an icon of late twentieth-century postmodern domestic architecture. Robert Venturi, with Denise Scott Brown, designed this house for his mother while he was still young. She had asked for comparative simplicity, yet did not want a modern house that would be incompatible with her antique furniture. This now-famous facade makes reference to classical architecture, but does so using overscaled elements. It has a skewed symmetry and is primarily an oversized gable with a chimney set slightly off-center, rising above it. The interior offers a similar mix; it fulfills familiar domestic expectations, while at the same time important elements, such as the fireplace and chimney, have a competitive rather than compatible relationship.

OLS HOUSE, 2011

Stuttgart, Germany

J. MAYER H. ARCHITECTS

Most of the houses in this hillside area date back to the 1960s and are of typical suburban design. This house, however, dramatically bucks this trend. Constructed of white reinforced concrete, the three-story dwelling features filleted corners and multiple angles which give it a sense of dynamism and futurism. The ground floor has a utility room and a spa, while the first has the living, dining, and kitchen areas, where full-height glazing provides a generous view of the valley; on the top floor are bedrooms. All are connected by a sculptural, ribbonlike central staircase. J. Mayer H.'s architecture can be characterized by his interest in biomorphic forms and use of concrete. The architect is known for his work in Georgia, including his extraordinary, amoebalike observation tower (2011) at the border with Turkey.

HOUSE P, 2015
Oberreute, Germany

YONDER ARCHITEKTUR
& DESIGN

Oberreute is a small town in Bavaria, known for its clean air. This holiday retreat's design is inspired by traditional Allgäu architecture—wooden chalets with pitched roofs and recessed balconies. Yonder took those elements and made them into a cuboid variation, metamorphosing the angles of a pitched roof into sloping walls. Wood is still an important material: flame-treated timber clads the exterior, while the interior features the most sumptuous untreated pale wood, giving the whole space a wonderful lightness and brightness. The three-story volume is built into a hillside, with an additional separate volume for storage. Between the two is a sheltered courtyard. In the dining/living room, an abstracted version of the typical Bavarian woodburning stove is the focus, but this one is fashioned of concrete.

HOUSE OF SILENCE, 2012

Nagahama, Shiga, Japan

FORM/KOUICHI KIMURA
ARCHITECTS

The House of Silence has a mute, almost hermetic facade. Sited on a residential street, it is designed to be free from its context. The project is framed by predominant planes of concrete which are counterbalanced by walls clad in shiny ceramic tiles. Behind the fortress-like exterior, interior rooms unfold from inner courtyards, with split-level plans creating rooms with a variety of ceiling heights. The heavy shell is perforated by elevated apertures visible in facades. Although they appear to be idiosyncratically located, they are in fact strategically placed to filter daylight inside, often through clerestory openings. The restrained palette of finishes seen on the exterior is repeated inside, with planes of concrete and tile forming desks, seating, and shelves which create a continuum between inside and outside.

CASA PEDREGAL, 1951

Mexico City, Mexico

LUIS BARRAGÁN

The area of El Pedregal in Mexico City is notable for its masses of black volcanic rock. It was the location for an experimental residential development conceived by Barragán in the 1940s. Barragán, who received the Pritzker Prize in 1980, attracted other leading architects to the project but designed this house for the Prieto family, and it is typical of his spare, planar compositional style. Textured pink walls juxtapose with the craggy lava outcrops, which also form part of the building's fabric inside. Former owners had turfed over much of the petrified lava, which was uncovered as part of a careful restoration of the property by current owner César Cervantes and architect Jorge Covarrubias in 2016. Overall, this project involves a sublime interplay between human habitation and nature.

TIMELINE

1901

p. 139

p. 262

p. 319

1902

p. 120

1903

p. 95

1904

p. 255

1905

p. 153

1907

p. 393

1908

p. 67

p. 239

p. 329

1909

p. 290

1910

p. 56

p. 79

p. 351

1911

p. 273

1913

p. 61

p. 249

1918

p. 211

1922

p. 97

p. 197

1924

p. 390

1926

p. 285

1929

p. 129

p. 232

p. 283

p. 322

p. 400

1930

p. 33

p. 223

p. 345

p. 352

1931

p. 68

p. 282

p. 151

p. 370

1932

p. 158

p. 185

1933

p. 113

1935

p. 286

1936

p. 16

p. 348

1937

p. 198

p. 284

p. 323

1938

p. 20

p. 55

p. 159

p. 330

1939

p. 72

p. 130

1941

p. 168

1946

p. 133

1947

p. 243

p. 334

1948

p. 336

1949

p. 212

p. 270

1950s & 60s

p. 321

1950

p. 69

p. 200

1951

p. 53

p. 236

p. 411

1952

p. 149

p. 171

1953

p. 18

p. 80

p. 83

p. 119

1954

p. 90

p. 364

1955

p. 150

p. 375

1956

p. 341

1957

p. 15

p. 32

p. 93

p. 132

p. 314

1958

p. 52

p. 92

1959

p. 75

p. 230

p. 297

1960s

p. 28

1960

p. 176

p. 192

1961

p. 76

1962

p. 30

p. 96

p. 121

p. 309

p. 383

p. 268

p. 320

p. 402

1963

p. 48

p. 276

p. 367

p. 380

1964

p. 180

p. 203

p. 407

1965

p. 35

p. 44

p. 172

p. 215

p. 359

p. 77

p. 294

p. 357

p. 398

p. 98

p. 304

1969

p. 45

1966

p. 19

p. 302

1968

p. 108

p. 71

1967

p. 167

p. 157

p. 170

1970

p. 99

p. 188

1971

p. 62

1972

p. 87

1973

p. 22

p. 57

p. 142

p. 305

p. 349

1974

p. 218

1975

p. 202

p. 228

p. 246

p. 382

1976

p. 49

p. 222

1976 (CONT'D)

1977

1978

1979

1982

1983

1984

1985

1986

p. 136

p. 358

1987

p. 205

1988

p. 81

p. 118

p. 178

p. 355

1989

p. 82

p. 214

p. 331

p. 374

1990

p. 144

p. 235

p. 241

1991

p. 37

p. 59

p. 64

p. 127

p. 146

1991 (CONT'D)

p. 340

p. 344

1992

p. 47

p. 54

p. 74

p. 311

p. 335

p. 386

1993

p. 138

p. 163

p. 227

1994

p. 85

p. 103

p. 191

p. 378

1995

p. 24

p. 126

p. 169

p. 209

p. 301

1996

p. 70

p. 253

p. 313

p. 405

1997

p. 152

p. 154

p. 300

p. 307

p. 354

p. 366

1998

p. 36

p. 88

p. 174

p. 177

p. 190

p. 245

p. 299

p. 384

1999

p. 201

p. 257

1999 (CONT'D)

2000

2001

2002

2003

2004

p. 376

2005

p. 17

p. 94

p. 107

p. 115

p. 131

p. 164

p. 298

p. 308

p. 315

p. 356

p. 373

p. 392

2006

p. 65

p. 105

p. 143

p. 145

p. 207

p. 208

p. 238

2006 (CONT'D)

p. 263

p. 306

2007

p. 13

p. 46

p. 114

p. 186

p. 216

p. 229

p. 242

p. 259

p. 272

p. 280

p. 395

2008

p. 43

p. 78

p. 155

p. 165

p. 189

p. 210

p. 244

2009

p. 269

p. 102

p. 254

p. 337

p. 333

p. 135

p. 258

p. 339

p. 338

p. 141

p. 264

p. 342

p. 372

p. 251

p. 287

p. 369

p. 397

p. 252

p. 332

p. 371

2009 (CONT'D)

p. 388

p. 391

2010

p. 104

p. 111

p. 162

p. 221

p. 250

p. 277

p. 292

p. 326

p. 328

p. 365

2011

p. 73

p. 109

p. 148

p. 179

p. 182

p. 194

p. 220

p. 234

2012

2013

p. 14

p. 25

p. 27

p. 39

p. 51

p. 63

p. 86

p. 100

p. 122

p. 125

p. 187

p. 247

p. 267

p. 289

p. 293

p. 347

2014

p. 34

p. 91

p. 110

p. 123

p. 237

p. 325

p. 60

p. 161

p. 256

p. 368

p. 66

p. 173

p. 275

p. 385

p. 117

p. 175

p. 288

2015

p. 140

p. 196

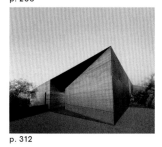

p. 312

p. 38

p. 147

p. 58

2018

INDEX

PICTURE CREDITS

Every reasonable effort has been made to acknowledge the ownership of copyright for photographers included in this volume. Any errors that may have occurred are inadvertent, and will be corrected in subsequent editions provided notification is sent in writing to the publisher.

Phaidon Press Limited
Regent's Wharf
All Saints Street
London N1 9PA

Phaidon Press Inc.
65 Bleecker Street
New York, NY 10012

phaidon.com

First Published in 2019
© 2019 Phaidon Press Limited

ISBN 978 0 7148 7809 6

A CIP catalogue record for this book
is available from the British Library and
the Library of Congress.

Commissioning Editor: Virginia McLeod
Project Editor: Belle Place
Production Controller: Sarah Kramer
Picture Researcher: Milena Harrison-Gray
Artworker: Christopher Lacy

Design: Hans Stofregen

Special thanks to Rachel Giles and Sam
Lubell for their contributions to the text.

The publisher would also like to thank
Vanessa Bird, Robert Davies, and Lisa
Delgado for their contributions to the book.

Printed in China